acher
eing in
dhood

**NEA
EARLY CHILDHOOD
EDUCATION SERIES**

# Parent-Teacher Conferencing in Early Childhood Education

S. Dianne Lawler

**A NATIONAL EDUCATION ASSOCIATION
PUBLICATION**

Copyright © 1991
National Education Association of the United States


Printing History
   First Printing:   October 1991

**Note**

The opinions expressed in this publication should not be construed as representing the policy or position of the National Education Association. This publication is intended as a discussion document for educators who are concerned with specialized interests of the profession.

**Library of Congress Cataloging-in-Publication Data**

Lawler, S. Dianne.
     Parent-teacher conferencing in early childhood education / S. Dianne Lawler.
          p.   cm.   —(NEA early childhood education series)
     Includes bibliographical references.
     ISBN O–8106–0356X
     1. Parent-teacher conferences. 2. Early childhood education—United States. I. Title. II. Series: Early childhood education series (Washington D.C.)
LC225.5.L37     1991
372.11'03—dc20                                          91–13090
                                                           CIP

# CONTENTS

**Author**

S. Dianne Lawler is Assistant Professor of Early Childhood Education at Arkansas State University, Jonesboro.

**The Advisory Panel**

Colleen Browning, Second Grade Teacher, Ocala Springs Elementary School, Ocala, Florida

Steve Hoppin, School Psychologist, Jefferson County Public Schools, Golden, Colorado

Richard W. Saxe, Distinguished Professor of Educational Leadership, The University of Toledo, Ohio

Marlene Zappia-Hall, Projects Coordinator, Creighton Elementary School District, Phoenix, Arizona

# Chapter 1

# THE LAWLER MODEL FOR EFFECTIVE PARENT-TEACHER CONFERENCES

## SITUATIONAL VIGNETTE: JASON CHILDERS

You are a first grade teacher at Westwood Elementary School. Fall conferences are approaching and you must organize and plan to meet with each parent.

Jason is six years and three months old. He is somewhat overweight, has difficulty pronouncing many words, and is very immature. Jason is thoughtful and always eager to help with classroom tasks. He is generous and sharing with the other children. He has few friends; most of the other children choose not to play with him. He moves slowly on the playground and doesn't participate in any active games during recess.

Your major concern is Jason's reading. He is having a great deal of difficulty with skills. His test scores on "magazine tests" have been low and his comprehension is poor.

You have noticed that school records indicate Jason's address is in a "bad" part of town. He talks frequently about living with "Mamaw and Papaw" (his grandparents), along with his mother. The note you sent home requesting times for the conference was signed by Jason's grandmother, so you expect her to attend the conference.

How will you approach these concerns about Jason's academic performance, as well as his social relationships with peers? How can you explain the results of the skills test to his grandmother? How can you talk about Jason's weight problem and its possible effects on his self-concept? Most importantly, how will you develop a partnership with Jason's family (with the person who attends the conference) to accomplish *all* these goals in educating Jason?

Why is the process of contacting parents an unresolved issue for teachers? Do teachers expect parents to react negatively? "Do they feel that the parents may be insulted or even deny the problem?" (13)* Are there lingering suspicions that parents may challenge teachers' competencies?

On the other hand, why do parents appear to shy away from teachers? "Are they afraid of causing trouble for their child if they mention a problem the teacher may not have noticed?" (13) Parents and professionals should work toward the goal of developing cooperative partnerships. These partnerships must be based on the premise that all positive, collaborative efforts are helpful to the child. Parents need more detailed information about the professionals with whom they will be interacting (13). Teachers must learn to lessen the parents' initial anxiety and possible negative feelings.

## CONFERENCE MODEL

The following model was designed to assist teachers in the process of interacting with parents, particularly in scheduled meetings. Although all conferences are different and there are no set answers, the model provides ideas to help teachers communicate effectively and establish partnerships with parents.

When meeting with parents, time is limited and in some cases both teacher and parent may be nervous and/or uncomfortable. The following guidelines may enable teachers to better prepare and work through problems in conferencing. To date, there are no models from which teachers can learn conferencing skills. This model is based on the literature concerning conferencing techniques and research on effective conferencing.

---

*Numbers in parentheses appearing in the text refer to the Bibliography beginning on page 103.

The author's previous teaching experience has also contributed significantly to the design.

## The Lawler Model*

L   *LOCATE* records, materials, etc., necessary for effectively interacting with parents.

A   *ARRANGE* the environment for a relaxed, pleasant atmosphere.

W   *WORK* toward "partnerships" with parents. (Do NOT dominate the conference!)

L   *LISTEN* more than 50 percent of the planned conference time.

E   *EVALUATE* the conference as it proceeds.

R   *RESPOND* to the parents in terms of followup.

The model will now be broken into parts to provide more specific guidelines for effective conferencing. Although unscheduled conferences cannot follow this model exactly, they may be improved through learning skills in effective conferencing. Additional information on communication skills, body language, physical environment, and types of followup responses for scheduled conferences will be included.

L *Locate* records, materials, etc., necessary for effectively interacting with parents.

1. Plan an agenda, selecting two to four priority goals for each child (5).
2. Send the agenda to parents with a note requesting time preferences for the conference.
3. Ask the parents if they have concerns to discuss (5).

A *Arrange* the environment for a relaxed, pleasant atmosphere.

4. Arrange the environment so that parents will feel

---

*Copyright 1990, S. Dianne Lawler, Assistant Professor, Early Childhood Education, Arkansas State University, Jonesboro.

comfortable. The room should be neat and orderly. Examples of children's work should be displayed attractively. Show the parents where their child sits, works, etc. (NOTE: Providing a small table and chair outside the classroom also supports the idea of comfort for parents who have to wait.)

5. Have adult-sized chairs in which the parents and you may sit.

6. Greet each parent at the door using *your* first name. Clarify parents' names with your records. Many children are from divorced, blended, and stepparent families today. All family members are not addressed by the same last name.

7. Sit beside or at an angle from the parent. *NEVER* sit behind your desk or at a table across from the parent. It is intimidating.


W *Work* toward partnerships with parents (do not dominate the conference).

8. Begin on a positive note. Think of something good to say about each child. (If you cannot think of anything positive to say about a particular child, ask colleagues for help. Be sure to begin on a positive note.)

9. Keep a notepad nearby and take notes. You cannot remember the suggestions/recommendations of all parents. Parents should also see that their input is important enough for you to record and utilize. (NOTE: If parents object to your writing comments, assure them it is for your benefit only, that conference discussions are confidential.)

10. Discuss educational plans and concerns.

11. Be clear and concise. Do not use jargon. (Even the names of tests—for example, MAT-6 [Metropolitan Achievement Test, Version 6]—should be explained.)

12. Do not talk down to parents. If you practice in front of a mirror and your eyebrows are never in a relaxed position, but are always raised, this is a sure sign that you are, indeed, talking in a condescending manner.

13. Base judgments on available *facts* from actual situations. Never repeat comments of other teachers or students to parents. Document behavior when discussing incidents. No one can be expected to relate detailed information concerning all students to all parents. Keep records.

14. Be constructive in all suggestions to parents (26). We know that parents consider their children extensions of themselves. When a teacher is criticizing the child, parents also feel criticized. Parents may often feel intimidated by teachers, regarding knowledge of parenting skills (or lack thereof). Teachers are the experts in the eyes of parents (generally). Be careful.

15. Offer more than one solution to a problem. Treat parents as adults by providing alternatives so that they may have specific input and feel that they contribute.


L *Listen* more than 50 percent of the planned conference time. The information gained *from* the parent is equally as important as the information you have to share.

16. Talk less than 50 percent of the scheduled time. You are a facilitator, not a director or dictator.

17. Listen carefully and paraphrase for clarification. If parents are intimidated and/or nervous, they may not express themselves well. While hearing back the message you received, they may realize that it was not the one they meant to send. Give them support and assistance in this interactive process through paraphrasing.

E    *Evaluate* the conference as it proceeds.

18. Make necessary adjustments in the agenda while conferencing.
19. Mentally ask yourself how the conference is proceeding.
20. Ask for and accept suggestions from parents. Some teachers are often afraid of what they might hear. Be open-minded and willing to listen and respond to parental suggestions. Remember, the parent has known the child much longer than you have known the child.


R    *Respond* to the parent in terms of followup.

21. Make *educational plans* for future accomplishment of goals and objectives. If parents are to become partners, they must be included in some way by making followup arrangements. When a conference ends and the parent is "dismissed" by the teacher, the parent often feels as if he/she is no longer needed and has no further part to play in the educational process. Parents come to school from many walks of life and, as in working with children, teachers must work with them on their levels. A single conference during the school year is not enough to develop a partnership with the parent.
22. Allow for parental input in *all* aspects of the child's education. Always make educational plans with the parents to *respond* to their needs and those of the child.
23. Summarize the key points of the conference.
24. Plan for followup communication. (This item is often omitted, but it is most important.) Never end a conference without planning what type of future

interaction will occur between you and the parent. Followup may consist of a note sent home, a note from the parent, a phone call, or (ideally) a face-to-face conference.

Now read what actually occurred during the Jason conference. Refer to the model to determine the effectiveness of the conference.

## CONFERENCE VIGNETTE: JASON CHILDERS

*Conference with Jason's Grandmother*

*Background.* The note was sent home, along with an agenda. Jason's grandmother signed the note, requested Thursday at 3 o'clock for her meeting time, and indicated no concerns to be discussed.

On Thursday at 3 o'clock Mrs. Walker (Jason's grandmother) arrives. You greet her at the door and introduce yourself as Jane. She enters the room and you comment that Jason has talked of Mamaw often and you are happy to meet her. You tour the room quickly and show her where Jason sits, some of the learning centers, and samples of Jason's work posted on the bulletin board.

You have arranged a table (your reading table) and four adult-sized chairs. Mrs. Walker seats herself in one of the chairs and you sit in a chair at an angle from her.

JANE: Mrs. Walker, I am so happy to meet with you. Jason is one of the most sharing and giving children I have taught.

MRS. WALKER: Well, thank you. He is a good boy at home, too.

JANE: I would like to begin by showing you some samples of

Jason's work and talking about his progress. (You have a file folder and discuss Jason's work, allowing Mrs. Walker to make comments and ask questions.)

JANE: The reading series we use is _____. In this series the children complete magazine tests. These are like unit tests and tell us whether the children are ready to move on to the next level. Jason has had some difficulty with these tests. His reading comprehension skills are weak. This is a problem in that he cannot remember what he has read, so he has difficulty answering the questions at the end of the story. Does Jason like to read at home?

MRS. WALKER: Well, he doesn't read, but he sure wants me to read to him a lot. Is that bad?

JANE: No. Reading to Jason is .great! I'm glad that he is interested in reading. Maybe you could try asking him some questions at the end of the story. You might also ask him to read a book to you. I ask the children to take library books home each week. You might ask him some questions after he has read the story to you.

MRS. WALKER: You know, Jason's mother works the night shift and he doesn't see her much. I try to do lots of things with him, but I have been out of school so long myself that I have a hard time remembering what little kids do at school. (She chuckles.)

JANE: Well, I'm sure that Jason likes to tell you about what we do and you probably remember from your daughter's schooling some of what she did. Jason tells me that you tell him wonderful stories. Maybe you could ask him some questions after you tell him a story. That might help improve his reading comprehension.

MRS. WALKER: OK. I think I could do that.

JANE: Tell me about Jason's eating and sleeping habits at home.

(You have a notepad and take notes as Mrs. Walker speaks. You don't try to hide these from her and let her see what you are writing. Mrs. Walker does not appear to be bothered or intimidated by this.)

MRS. WALKER: He sure does like to eat. He goes to bed about 9 o'clock and gets up at 6:30 so I can feed him breakfast and have him ready to get on the schoolbus by 7:30.

JANE: What kinds of foods does he like?

MRS. WALKER: Well, he eats biscuits and gravy for breakfast. And you know he eats in the cafeteria at lunchtime. He has a snack when he gets home and we eat supper around 6:30 when his Papaw gets home.

JANE: What does he usually eat for his snack?

MRS. WALKER: He has cookies and sometimes a piece of bread with cheese or butter. Is that bad?

JANE: No. I was just interested in what Jason does at home. He does seem to like the cafeteria food and usually eats most of his food. The school nurse weighed and measured the children last week and Jason seemed a little embarrassed.

MRS. WALKER: He really is big! But then, his Papaw and I are sort of fat, too. Do you think he needs to go on a diet?

JANE: I don't know that you would want to put Jason on a structured diet. Maybe more exercise would help him burn calories. Does Jason play outside much at home?

MRS. WALKER: Not much. He really likes to be with me in the house, especially in the kitchen.

JANE: Maybe you could encourage him to play outside more at home and I will encourage him to play in more active games with the other boys and girls. Maybe if he gets more exercise he will grow taller and healthier.

MRS. WALKER: I don't know much about diets. I've never been on one myself.

JANE: If you'd like, I'll ask the nurse to send home some nutrition information about food groups, calories, etc.?

MRS. WALKER: OK.

JANE: Mrs. Walker, our time is almost up. Let's see. We have talked about Jason's sharing attitude. We discussed his reading comprehension and talked about ways we could both work on this. We also discussed his eating patterns and exercise. Are there any other questions or items you would like to discuss?

MRS. WALKER: Not now. I'll probably get home and think of some, though. (She chuckles again.)

JANE: I would really like to meet with you again before our spring conference time. I'll send a note or call when I feel I have more information to share with you. Would you call me or send a note when you would like to talk?

MRS. WALKER: Yes and I'll tell Jason's mother what you said. She may want to talk with you too. Could you meet with her early in the morning sometime?

JANE: Yes, as long as the children have not arrived. Maybe she could come around 7:30 some morning. Send a note with Jason the day before, if possible, and I'll arrange for another teacher to supervise the children while we meet.

MRS. WALKER: Thank you.

JANE: It has been nice to talk with you. I can see where Jason gets his pleasant disposition. I look forward to working with you, Mrs. Walker.

## CONCLUSIONS

Although this is a fictitious circumstance, it is similar to some you may encounter at any grade level. Once again, all conferences differ because of agendas, children's behaviors and/or academic performance; the background of the parents and their communication styles; the teacher's experience, planning, communication style, and personality; as well as the comfort zone of both parent and teacher during the meeting.

The following chapter discusses the research on parental backgrounds and the influence of this factor on parental attitudes and reactions to teachers as well as to conferences.

Chapter 2

# RESEARCH ON PARENTAL ATTITUDES AND INTERACTIONS WITH TEACHERS

Teacher Talk:
Summary of Research

1. Parents need and want to conference with teachers (68).
2. Teachers believe parental involvement is important (68).
3. Parental involvement in the classroom helps increase involvement in children's learning activities at home (37).
4. Parents and teachers (generally) appear to have the same goals for children (37).
5. High school graduates appear to be the most active group in parent involvement (67).
6. Higher socioeconomic status (SES) parents were more involved in and aware of school activities (30).
7. Sixty-two percent of teachers surveyed believe parents leave their children alone too much after school (27).
8. The majority of teachers did NOT feel that parents exhibit *lack of respect* for teachers (27).
9. Teachers prefer to meet with parents during the school day or immediately after school (27).
10. Many parents prefer evening meetings due to work schedules (27).

This research tells us that, although there may not be complete agreement on all issues between parents and teachers, there is consensus on goals and ideas. It also tells us that teachers must be cautious about making value judgments concerning parents, their parental styles, their methods of discipline and child care, and their level of participation in school activities. This body of research also provides us with parents' perspectives.

As teachers, we must make that extra effort if the partnerships with parents are to work. In our changing society, more and more parents work outside the home. We must begin to recognize and accommodate these parents so that quality education and equal partnerships may be established between home and school.

## RATIONALE FOR CONFERENCING

### Teacher Talk:
### Summary of Research

1. Parental support can be a vital factor in children's achievement (58).
2. The Southwest Educational Development Laboratory (SEDL) found that (a) an increase in parent involvement should occur; (b) teachers should confer with parents about home life; (c) parents would help children at home if they knew what to do (58).
3. Many times conferences are scheduled *only* when there is a problem (50).
4. Parents chiefly receive information about school from their children and they *prefer* to receive information from them (46).
5. Parents appear to shy away from face-to-face interactions with teachers at school (54).
6. Generally, teachers are *not* properly trained to conduct conferences with parents effectively (58).

This research tells us that parents are important in the process of educating young children. Parents want to help in this process but often do not know how to do so in appropriate ways. They seem to shy away from meeting with teachers. Perhaps they feel intimidated. They also may feel that they are on the teachers' turf. Finally, the research has indicated that teachers have not generally been trained to conduct effective conferences.

Look at the following conference between Mrs. Carlson and Mark Bryan's mother. See what happens in a poorly conducted meeting when two people are not communicating well.

## SITUATIONAL VIGNETTE:
## MARK BRYAN*

Mark is a third grader. His academic work is satisfactory except in mathematics. In addition, he is not as responsible as most of the children in doing independent library work. Lately, he has been a bit of a discipline problem. He disrupted a small group session by maintaining unrelated side conversations, was caught running through the Materials Resource Center, and it was reported that he vandalized a learning center.

Mrs. Bryan and her husband are professionals. They have very high aspirations for Mark. Both tend to project their personalities and personal aspirations on Mark. Mrs. Bryan thinks that whatever subject areas were difficult for her in school will also be difficult areas for Mark. Basically, she will not accept any suggestions or recommendations, and refuses to believe that there are any problem areas.

### Conference Vignette:
### Mark Bryan

Mrs. Carlson, Mark Bryan's third grade teacher, is conducting scheduled fall conferences to discuss academic performance and progress. She has the room arranged neatly with a reading table and adult-sized chairs. However, her materials and her chair are behind the table. She prefers to sit across from the parent. She believes it gives her the edge in discussions and in making points about what she wants parents to accomplish with their children. She has remained on schedule throughout the day.

---

*Adapted from "Simformation 6: Planning, Conducting, and Evaluating Parent-Teacher Conferences," by R. Cooper and others. National Institute of Education, Washington, D.C., 1977. ED 208 466.

It is 4:30 and she has two more (20-minute) conferences before leaving the building. Mrs. Bryan arrives.

MRS. CARLSON: Hello, Mrs. Bryan. I am glad that you could come to discuss Mark's progress. Boy! He's a problem! But then, I really have my hands full. This is the worst third grade class I've had in years.

MRS. BRYAN: Mrs. Carlson, I certainly hope that you are NOT saying that Mark is a problem. Mr. Bryan and I are both attorneys and hope to put Mark through law school, too. He'll need a high GPA to be admitted to Yale. That's where his father received his degree, you know.

MRS. CARLSON: (She has her file folder open. She looks at her documentation to report what has happened concerning Mark's behavior.) Well, basically, Mark has been a troublemaker lately. During the last few weeks he has gotten into a fight with a boy in the quiet study areas, he was accused by one girl of vandalizing a learning center, he has disrupted a small group session by instigating and maintaining unrelated side conversations, and he was belligerent when I reprimanded him for running through the Materials Resource Center.

MRS. BRYAN: Oh, well, boys will be boys. Actually, I don't see what his behavior has to do with his academic performance. Now, how were his math grades? I wasn't very strong in math.

MRS. CARLSON: Well, Mark's behavior *is* related to his academic performance and, honestly, he's just lazy. Lately, he has been uncooperative, disinterested in school, turning in a poor grade of work, and fails to hand in outside assignments. (She is reading this, once again, from her documentation.)

MRS. BRYAN: What? Now, tell me what these outside assignments are.

MRS. CARLSON: Well, Mark has not been handing in homework and when I question him about it he says that he doesn't have a place to study at home where he can put out his materials and work quietly. You realize that if he doesn't hand in these outside assignments, he *will* be retained this year. You see, we have no control over his life at home and I can't make him do his homework.

MRS. BRYAN: Well, I'm certain that Mark just doesn't understand these outside assignments *you* give, or he would complete his homework. He's probably just bored, you know. He *is* extremely bright. I'm certain that the work he *does* turn in is of very high quality.

MRS. CARLSON: Well, Mrs. Bryan, if I were you I'd be checking on Mark's home study habits. Now, I believe our time is up and that my next appointment is waiting. Thank you for your time.

## CONCLUSIONS

Few, if any, teachers would conference like Mrs. Carlson. This adapted version from the literature provides an example of poor communication between a teacher and a parent. Actually, the two conference participants did not communicate.

All teachers have had groups of children who challenge them. They should not, however, relate these feelings to parents. Teachers must take the responsibility for each child, as well as the whole group. The vignette also showed that Mrs. Carlson reminisced about the good old days when parents were more responsible. She made assumptions about the Bryans' not being responsible in parenting skills. She placed blame on the parents for Mark's academic performance and his being prevented from going on to the next grade level.

Mrs. Bryan began the conference arrogantly. She projected her goals and aspirations on Mark. She discussed the distant future (Mark entering Yale) but not the immediate future. She disregarded the difficult behavior the teacher discussed. She dismissed the academic problems by defending Mark and saying that because he was so bright, he was probably bored. She became concerned about the outside assignments, but when she learned that Mark blamed his work environment at home, she defended her child saying, "I'm certain that if he understood them, he would complete them." Mrs. Bryan blamed the teacher. She asked no further questions, nor did she make plans for further discussion with Mrs. Carlson. The teacher, too, made no effort for future plans, goals, or meetings.

Communication is the key to an effective conference with parents. Although everyone has a different communication style and teachers cannot control parent responses, efforts to communicate openly and effectively are essential. The following chapter provides information concerning communication skills that should help teachers in their meetings with parents.

# Chapter 3

# COMMUNICATION

Research has indicated that teachers are not adequately prepared for effective communication with parents (13, 14, 37, 66). "To make individual conferences productive, careful advance planning, good communication skills, and willingness to collaborate are required" (61). It is wise for teachers to include not only a discussion of papers, achievement, and accomplishments, but also an ancedote or two that communicate a vivid picture of the uniqueness of the child. To bring about effective conferences, teachers must use effective listening skills, be aware of body language, provide appropriate feedback, be able to resolve conflicts, and create a climate for collaboration.

Norton described these communicator style variables:

- *Friendly*—The friendly communicator is encouraging to people, acknowledges others' contributions, openly expresses admiration and respect, and tends to be tactful.
- *Relaxed*—The relaxed communicator is calm and collected, not nervous under pressure, and does not show nervous mannerisms.
- *Attentive*—The attentive communicator likes to listen to the other person, shows interest in what the other is saying, and deliberately reacts in such a way that the other knows s/he is being heard.
- *Animated*—The animated communicator provides frequent and sustained eye contact, uses many facial expressions, and gestures often.
- *Impression Leaving*—The impression-leaving communicator tends to be remembered because of stimuli she or he projects.

- *Open*—The open communicator readily reveals personal information about self in communicative interactions.
- *Dramatic*—The dramatic communicator manipulates exaggerations, fantasies, stories, rhythm, voice, and other stylistic devices to highlight or understate content.
- *Precise*—The precise communicator tries to be strictly accurate when arguing, prefers well-defined arguments, and likes proof or documentation when arguing.
- *Dominant*—The dominant communicator talks frequently, takes charge in a social situation, comes on strong, and controls informal conversations.
- *Contentious*—The contentious communicator is argumentative (49).

These styles help us look at effective and ineffective methods of communicating with parents. Although some traits are positive in conferencing techniques (for example, friendly, relaxed, attentive, animated, and open), others may hinder the exchange of information and prevent partnerships with parents from becoming established (for example, overly dramatic, precise, dominant, and contentious). Each parent-teacher conference is different. The interplay of parent and teacher behaviors during the meeting determines the success or failure of the conference (10). A skillful teacher interacts in such a way that educational plans are made and goals are accomplished. A teacher who conducts effective meetings recognizes different parent interaction styles and modifies his/her behavior appropriately.

Reiss observes that "to be fully involved partners, parents must view themselves as having equal status with educators" (56). While conferencing with parents, invite positive feelings by carefully choosing your language and terminology. Many

28

teachers assume the role of expert during the conference (35). It is important to consider conferences as "collaborative consultations." Such consultation could be described as an interactive process that enables people with diverse expertise to generate solutions to mutually defined problems (36). When teachers act as consultants to parents, they must become aware of barriers that may prevent effective interaction. Using technical terms and educational jargon may irritate and confuse parents. Littleton recommended avoiding "educationese" (42). Some of the most mistrusted physicians and attorneys are those who use terminology and jargon that laypeople do not understand.

To determine whether you are using jargon or educationese, obtain permission from a parent you know well and feel comfortable with to tape record the conference. Play it back and listen to yourself. You may not use language that is too technical, particularly with a parent with whom you feel comfortable, but you may use language you are unaware of, or that you had not planned to use. This practice could also assist you in evaluating yourself (see Appendix A) and in planning future conferences.

Remember, you are the facilitator of the discussion, but should not dominate. Although parents want to know about their children's activities, behavior, and performance, this information can be shared in the course of discussion rather than through a lengthy explanation (40). The emphasis should be on dialogue. Parents should not be viewed as threats, but as people of prime importance in the education of the young child. They must feel respected, valued, and appreciated. The teacher must develop through speaking a "we-ness" in the conference (1). The exchange of information between parents and teachers may take place only when listening skills are used by the teacher.

## LISTENING SKILLS

Effective communication is the most essential ingredient in the success of parent-teacher conferences (11). Although the benefits of effective conferences are recognized, many teachers often lack confidence in this area (12). If you are a dynamic, enthusiastic teacher, dominating the conversation may come easily to you (9). You may need to hone your listening skills.

Listening is a four-step process. It involves hearing, interpreting, evaluating, and responding (55). Although the sequencing of these processes is similar to the steps in the Lawler Model, they are a part of the listening phase of the model. While meeting with parents, listening involves not only hearing, but the other three elements also. "Being a good listener requires concentration, effort, and a willingness to give credence to what another is saying" (26).

Teachers need to examine their attitudes concerning the helpfulness with which they prejudge parental input. If they feel that scheduled parent-teacher conferences (or unscheduled ones as well) are a waste of time, they will find themselves concentrating on what they plan to say next, rather than on what the parent is trying to communicate to them.

Active listening and reflection are important tools in the flow of information between parents and teachers. When the teacher recognizes that the conference is a sharing process, half the burden has been lifted from his/her shoulders. Active listening means, literally, being active in the listening process. The receiver of information is concentrating on the message, making mental notes about the sender's purpose, thoughts, and intent. Active listening also involves paraphrasing and repeating the important parts of the message received. This enables the sender to hear the message that was received. The sender may hear it differently from the way he or she intended to send it. The sender may also determine that the listener interpreted the message in a different way from the one intended. Through active listening, and especially through paraphrasing, the messages that are sent and received throughout the conference may be more accurate, better understood, and more pleasant (relaxed and comfortable).

Reflective listening involves an awareness of open and closed responses. Maintaining an open, respectful flow of ideas requires the practice of reflective listening. Open responses invite continued dialogue; closed responses require little elaboration or thought. Closed responses often stop further discussion or information exchange between participants. Here are some examples of open and closed responses in conferences between parents and teachers (11).

Closed Response

>PARENT: I'm concerned about John's progress in math.
>TEACHER: If John would work harder, he would not have a problem.

Open Response

>PARENT: I'm concerned about John's progress in math.
>TEACHER: You are worried about John's progress in math?

Closed Response

>TEACHER: I'm concerned about John's progress in math.
>PARENT: That's your job. Can't you teach him?

Open Response

>TEACHER: I'm concerned about John's progress in math.
>PARENT: You are worried about John falling behind in math?

## INTERPRETING, EVALUATING, AND RESPONDING TO PARENTS

The communication process involves the exchange of information between parents and teachers in the conference setting. Aspects of the communication process that are often overlooked or ignored are the interpretation and evaluation of

31

the messages sent. One must concentrate, listen, think, interpret, evaluate, and respond to the sender of the message. The following example* depicts how the listening needs of a parent can be met (26).

TEACHER: David is very quiet in school. He doesn't usually participate in group discussions unless called upon. His responses, then, are usually brief.

PARENT: I wish I were that lucky. At home he talks all the time. Sometimes I am so tired after work and he is talking all the time; I have to ask him to be quiet for just a few minutes.

TEACHER: That may be because you know David better than I and because David is more comfortable at home with you. You haven't had the opportunity to see how David's behavior compares with children his own age at school. When I looked at David's records, I noticed that David's teacher from last year made similar observations.

PARENT: Yes, his teacher did say something about that. I guess I should be doing something for David.

In this example the teacher is concentrating, listening, interpreting, evaluating, and responding to the parent. It appears that some solutions will be agreed upon between this teacher and this parent from the direction their conversation is taking.

## CLARIFYING PARENT MESSAGE

It is also important to allow parents to clarify their thoughts and suggestions. Teachers must listen, interpret, and allow parents multiple opportunities to express themselves (many parents may not be as practiced at sending verbal messages as

---

*Adapted from "Focus on Parent-Teacher Conferences," by A. L. Hamachek and L. G. Rotter, 1984. ED 265 131.

teachers are). The following example* portrays, once again, the verbal messages between parent and teacher, and the teacher's ability to "think, listen, interpret, evaluate, and respond" while meeting with the parent (26).

TEACHER: What kinds of stories do you think Kaitlin would be interested in having read to her?

MOTHER: She likes some stories, but she likes space stories best.

TEACHER: I didn't know that. I have some books about space. Motivation and interest are two important factors in promoting a positive attitude toward reading. Although I want us to talk about how we can help Kaitlin correctly pronounce more words that are used in her reader, I would like her to receive the consistent message that reading is fun, she will learn to read, and reading is a purposeful activity.

MOTHER: What do you mean by purposeful activity?

TEACHER: It is really important that you and I ask each other questions. I'm glad you asked me that. I used "purposeful" to mean that reading is important in all our education and that everyone should read.

This example shows a teacher who is tuned in to the mother's messages and concerns. The teacher responds to the mother and her lack of understanding. Although it should be noted that "purposeful activity" may fit in the category of jargon, the teacher corrected her verbal error through further explanation without talking down to the parent. The teacher also reinforced the parent's clarification question. It appears that greater communication and further discussion concerning Kaitlin's needs and development will occur.

---

*Adapted from "Focus on Parent-Teacher Conferences," by A. L. Hamachek and L. G. Rotter, 1984. ED 265 131.

Another helpful quality in the communication process is the ability to sense what parents want from you. Most parents want to be assured that their child's teacher has the knowledge, ability, and willingness to see their child as a unique individual. Most parents can accept that you (the teacher) will observe both the strengths and weaknesses of their child, but they hope that you will recognize these objectively. Parents hope that you will support their child during times of stress (family illness, the arrival of a new baby, emotional strife). Parents appreciate a teacher who makes each child feel special—one who gives warm assistance, while holding the child accountable for learning. You can assure parents that you are all they expect from a teacher through effective communication in conferencing (9).

## THE CONFERENCE ENVIRONMENT

The atmosphere established throughout the conference will also influence the interaction occurring during the meeting. The environment may affect positive and negative responses from parents.

In the Lawler Model, "A" represents "Arranging the physical environment." The physical environment and the personal atmosphere should be considered in conferencing with parents. The primary consideration in selecting an appropriate meeting place is to create an atmosphere that will enhance communication (35). The classroom should be welcoming and inviting. A comfortable atmosphere means providing adult-sized chairs, hospitality, and possibly offering refreshments (even if they consist of a pitcher of ice water and paper cups) (44). Never sit behind a desk. A table provides a more relaxed setting, and promotes team effort from both participants. It is important for the parent to feel as important as the teacher. Ensure privacy by closing the door or arranging for sound barriers to be erected (8).

The personal atmosphere includes factors such as

greeting the parent at the door, rather than remaining in your seat; conveying a warm personal attitude while maintaining professionalism; and keeping the atmosphere pleasant, relaxed, and unhurried even when crucial issues arise (8). It is also important to be sensitive to the social and emotional needs of parents by talking with them, not at them. Enthusiasm for the activity in which you are engaged (conferencing) also conveys a personal message that you are interested in your job, the children, and that you consider the meeting important for future accomplishment of goals and objectives.

Although fatigue and burnout may set in after hours of conferencing, it is important to schedule the conferences so that your personal needs can be met too. You may need to systematically schedule time periods for breaks so that you can freshen up, stretch, and relax. It would be unfair to parents who are scheduled near the end of your conference day to receive less attention, enthusiasm, and effort than those scheduled at the beginning of the day when you are fresh and rested.

During scheduled conference meeting days it will probably be necessary and desirable to meet in your own classroom. When scheduling special meetings, followup conferences, or other meetings in which you would like to make parents feel equality, you may choose to confer in a neutral location (for example, the library or a conference room) (35). You may find that this alternative location provides a more neutral atmosphere and relaxed comfort for both parents and you.

While conferencing, it is important to stay focused on conversation and messages from parents. This is difficult when there are so many parents to see during the scheduled conference times. It is also physically taxing to shift gears so frequently (often in 20-minute intervals) and discuss a different child, different strengths and weaknesses, and different problem areas with each parent. It is helpful to stand up, escort the parent out, and welcome the incoming parent.

## BODY LANGUAGE

During the conferencing process, body language and your physical appearance are other important factors in effective communication. It is assumed that you will be appropriately dressed according to school policy, well groomed, and take pride in your personal appearance. These aspects of impressions you give parents are important. Your posture should be straight and tall while sitting and standing. This indicates pride in oneself. Your eye contact, body responses, and gestures will also influence the verbal messages you send and receive.

While sitting beside or at an angle from the parent, it is important to maintain eye contact at all times. Some parents who have low self-esteem, or who are from a culture different from yours, may not feel comfortable with close scrutiny. It is acceptable to look at notes, make notes, and look elsewhere periodically, but eye contact is a must when sending verbal messages to the parent. It is also helpful when concentrating on the message being sent to you by the parent.

Your body language, whether it is forward leaning or arms folded, also gives nonverbal messages to parents. If your arms are folded, you lean away from the parent, and have a strained expression on your face, chances are the parent will receive very negative nonverbal messages from you. This may also affect the verbal messages they receive from you. Negative body language may influence some of your positive verbal messages about the child and the child's progress.

Gesturing is something that most people do naturally, but it can also be distracting to the receiver of a verbal message. Practice in front of a mirror to see if your gesturing while talking is distracting. You may also discover monotonous habits in gesturing that you want to correct or alleviate.

Although the teacher has the primary responsibility for planning, organizing, and conducting the conference, parents bring their own backgrounds to the meeting as well. Parents make up a diverse group. Each has thoughts, beliefs, traditions, feelings, and ideas concerning the education of their children. To deal effectively with parents of young children in today's society, it is important to examine the changes in family structure. The following chapter examines these changes and their effects on teachers' relationships with parents in diverse families.

Chapter 4

# CHANGING FAMILY STRUCTURES

Today, and in the future, schools face the burden of educating students who have many potential problems (33). Demographic changes in society are occurring with unprecedented speed. The following trends can be anticipated during the 1990s:

1. Demographic shifts in population due to increases in the number of children, a large share of whom will be Black or Hispanic;
2. Changes in the context of childhood, suggesting the need to prepare children to adapt to and cope with future complexities and uncertainties;
3. Tension related to instructional issues; and
4. Increased concern about the quality of teaching and the effectiveness of educational programs (65).

A dramatic increase in the number of young children to be served by schools will occur in the next decade. A larger proportion of these children will be from lower socioeconomic backgrounds or members of minority groups. Because of the increase in the number of mothers employed outside the home, teachers and schools have become increasingly important sources of stability in children's lives. According to Hofferth, "Over the past two decades the proportion of children living with two parents has fallen dramatically, while the proportion living with only their mother has more than doubled" (32). The proportion of children under age six with employed mothers is expected to reach two-thirds by 1995, while the proportion of school-aged children with employed mothers may rise to three-fourths over the next ten years.

A great deal of research has been conducted to

understand the effects of parental divorce and separation (32). Researchers have concluded that divorce reduces children's school achievement, chances of high school graduation, and completed years of schooling (24, 28, 31, 44). Maternal employment, however, has neither positive nor negative effects on children (33).

Research has consistently shown that children born to teenage mothers are disadvantaged compared with those born to older mothers. One of these disadvantages is poor academic achievement (32). It has also been noted that poor children receive significantly less adequate medical care than other children. Consequently, poor health is more common among low-income children who are more likely to be Black and live in a one-parent family headed by the mother. (A resulting consequence of this is school absence.)

Additionally, children may not receive adult guidance and support in schools. As Holland points out, "School organization and management are designed to facilitate a focus on academic content rather than to promote desirable staff-student interactions and adequate student growth and development" (33).

## TYPES OF FAMILIES

There are many types of families. In past years, it was acceptable to discuss the family as a "nuclear unit"—consisting of two parents and one or more children. Although this may be the preferred family unit, it is no longer the one in which many children live. Consideration must be given, not only during learning time, but before and during interactions with parents, to family structures.

The extended family consists of parents, grandparents, aunts, uncles, brothers, sisters, and sometimes cousins, living together as a unit. "Children may be reared by any other family members, particularly grandparents" (48). Unfortunately, sometimes when a grandparent responds to a note or request for a parent-teacher conference, an unperceptive teacher interprets this as a sign that the parents don't care. In the extended family, the primary role of the grandparent may be to respond, cooperate, and assist in the educative process.

Single-parent families are increasing rapidly. This increase includes a large number of single fathers rearing dependent children. The implications for the school are clear. More interested, involved, and caring fathers will be visiting the school, some by choice with the mother, others—single fathers—will participate alone (43).

Conferencing with fathers is not unlike meetings with mothers. The father's position may be somewhat uncomfortable, however. His role may have shifted from focus on other matters to primary responsibility for the education of the children.

Stepfamilies and blended families constitute another variation in family structure. Morrison defines a stepfamily as "one parent with the children of his or her own and a spouse" (48). A "blended," merged, or reconstructed family is one in which two people, each with children of their own, marry and combine families. One major consideration in conferencing with parents in this category is that last names of various family members may or *may not* change. Members within the household may be addressed by different last names. When conferencing with parents (singly or in couples), be sure to address them by the appropriate last name.

Another type of nontraditional family is made up of foster parents and children. Morrison defines foster parents as "those who care for, in a family setting, children who are not their own" (48). These parents are usually screened by agencies who place children with them. Sometimes the children are relatives. The children remain with foster parents for various periods of time and are occasionally adopted by them. Foster parents may not have much background information about the child. They may be anxious to cooperate and help, but unable to provide clear answers or explanations about the child.

Wardle notes that "the number of interracial marriages has increased to more than 100,000 in the past decade" (64). The U.S. census reports 632,000 interracial marriages in 1983; 125,000 were Black/white unions (42). According to Ladner (38), parents of interracial children tend to deal with the racial and ethnic identity of their children in one of three ways:

1. Some parents say their child is a human being above all else—color is totally irrelevant;
2. Other parents teach their children to have Black identity, or the identity of color, and to learn minority survival skills;
3. Another group teaches its children that they are interracial and should have an interracial identity.

It is important for teachers to understand these types of identity patterns. Teachers should consult with the parents about the child's heritage and ask how to handle it, realizing that parents of interracial children are often particularly sensitive to racism. As Wardle points out, "While all families of young children are under pressure, interracial couples feel additional kinds of pressures" (64).

Teachers, exhibiting their best efforts—without expressions of appreciation—often respond in defensive ways (33). This is understandable. They may say and feel, "The parents don't care." They defend this reaction by providing evidence that parents don't keep appointments or attend school functions. At the same time, however, most parents do care; they have difficulty interacting with the school.

Holland cautions that "differences between home and school—whether of class, race, income, or culture—always create potential conflict" (33). Since schools are no longer a natural part of the community, the union between home and school must be forged. In addition, whenever there is a conflict between groups who must relate to one another to achieve a goal, the group with the most power must usually make the most efforts to overcome obstacles in order to create desirable relationships.

These changes in demographics and family structure will affect the interactions that occur between home and school. Teachers must be better prepared than ever before to deal with these changes. If effective partnerships between home and school are to develop, teachers must be cognizant of families, societal changes, trends in families and politics, and willing to accept these changes. Moreover, teachers need to be more assertive in efforts to promote positive relations with parents for optimal learning to occur for all children.

Early childhood professionals are faced with additional challenges through the various family structures. The ultimate goal is to be sensitive to and supportive of the unique needs of each group, working closely and cooperatively with each family.

The following conference vignette examines what happened when a single-parent (mother) met with an inexperienced, unprepared male teacher concerning a sensitive issue.

## SITUATIONAL VIGNETTE: SUJETTE

Sujette is one of the most outgoing second graders Kevin Lindsay has ever seen. Last week one of the children reported that Sujette opened her blouse for the boys to see. She is always dressing up and pretending to put on makeup. She talks about boyfriends constantly, about kissing, going out on dates, and having babies. Kevin has called Sujette's mother in for a meeting about this situation. This is their first meeting, and Mr. Lindsay is quite nervous about how to describe Sujette's behavior. He tries to approach the issue gently.

Now read what happens. Ms. Martin has been notified that she should attend, but has been given no reason for the conference except that "There is a problem." Scheduled conferences have not occurred, so Ms. Martin is anxious to understand what Sujette could have done.

*Conference Vignette: Sujette**

TEACHER: Ms. Martin, I am Kevin Lindsay, Sujette's teacher here in the second grade. I am so glad that you could come for this conference.

MS. MARTIN: Well, when you said that there was some kind of problem, I was so concerned that I changed my busy schedule. Just exactly what is the problem?

TEACHER: Um, well . . . You see, I'm not even sure how to talk to you about this. I, um, well, I don't, um, know, um, how to explain this to you. (He is stammering around.) Well, I'm kind of worried about Sujette's behavior, um . . .

MS. MARTIN: (Interruping) Now, wait! She has always been a well-behaved child. I can't *believe* that she's actually a discipline problem! Not my Sujette, no way! What did she do, anyway?

TEACHER: It's not exactly a discipline problem or anything like that. It's just that . . . um . . . . Well, I'm worried about Sujette's future. You see, she seems kind of, well, more "grown up" than some of the other children. She talks about boyfriends a lot, and uh . . .

MS. MARTIN: (Interrupting again) Oh, isn't that cute! Everybody tells me that Sujette is just like me! You know, I was captain of the varsity cheerleading squad when I was in school. I had such a great time! In fact, I dated every ONE of the varsity football players during my senior year. Of course, I was also homecoming queen and voted most popular of the senior class. Oh, it was great! Those were the best years of my life. I just HOPE that Sujette has as much fun. You don't mean that her talking about boyfriends is the problem, here, do you?

---

*Adapted from "Sujette Conference Role-Play Activity." Based on materials prepared by J. P. Bauch, Peabody College of Vanderbilt University, Nashville, Tenn., 1985.

TEACHER: Oh, well. No. It . . . um . . . isn't . . . um . . . just that. You see . . . um . . . well . . . she even talks about getting married and having babies.

MS. MARTIN: (Interrupting a third time) Nooo! Isn't that cute! Ha! Ha! (Laughing) That girl! She really is just like her mother! You know, she always watches me put on my makeup and watches me put the henna in my hair. Sometimes, I even buy her clothes that match mine, and she looks just darlin'. You see, Mr. Lindsay, I am awfully happy with my life, and I want Sujette to be *just the same.* I hope she has lots of boyfriends and gets to go to all the parties. I sure did!

TEACHER: Well, that's nice, Ms. Martin, but I think that Sujette's behavior is going to lead to trouble. The real reason I called you is because of something that happened on Wednesday. Um . . . Let's see, now. Um . . . Well, what happened was that . . . um . . . well, she . . . um . . . opened her blouse and let the boys look at her chest.

MS. MARTIN: (Laughing) What? You're telling me that *my little girl* let the boys see her chest? Ha! Ha! Surely you know that little girls in second grade don't have anything to show. Why, they look just like the boys, although I hope that changes and she turns out like me. You CAN'T be serious! What did the little boys say?

TEACHER: Well . . . um . . . they said that Sujette showed them her "teddies."

MS. MARTIN: (Laughing) What, teddies? How cute. I can't wait to tell my friends. Isn't that precious? Is this what you called me here for? To tell me that my little girl is *promiscuous?* Surely you can't be serious. She's just a little girl. Besides, she sure seems to be learning how to be popular with the boys. That girl is going to have so much fun! Just wait 'til I tell everyone at the hair salon. (She leaves the room.)

# CONCLUSIONS

Mr. Lindsay was unprepared and, obviously, quite nervous. He did not have proper documentation for this conference. The issue discussed here has been debated in various in-service sessions, but considering that young children have a natural curiosity about anatomy and that the incident occurred only once, Mr. Lindsay should never have called Ms. Martin in to discuss this "problem." He should have handled the minor incident, possibly reporting it to the principal so that he/she would have been aware that it occurred (in the event that other parents called the school about it), and made proper documentation.

Mr. Lindsay also attempted to project his own beliefs and feelings on Ms. Martin and Sujette. He was judgmental. He called Ms. Martin, causing her anxiety, but did not provide her with any information concerning the conference except to alert her that there was an existing problem. This was unfair to the parent. Although it is ineffective to attempt to solve a problem by telephone, it should be discussed briefly to help parents collect their thoughts, become accustomed to the idea that a problem exists, and prepare possible solutions before meeting face-to-face with the teacher.

Mr. Lindsay was not clear and concise. When conferencing, he should have been prepared, maintained a calm, poised attitude, and attempted to pull the mother back on track. He seemed to encircle the subject. Not only did he fail to suggest more than one solution, he offered no solutions. This conference should never have taken place.

## The Defensive Parent

Ms. Martin was very busy explaining her personal position to Mr. Lindsay and did not appear upset by his concerns about Sujette. She was defensive about Sujette being a "discipline problem," since this had not occurred before. She became defensive when she interpreted Mr. Lindsay's accusations about Sujette as labeling her "promiscuous." What parent would not react negatively to such an accusation? This parent, particularly, tended to project her own beliefs, personality, and lifestyle on her daughter. Ms. Martin left the conference to spread the news of the cuteness of Sujette's behavior to her friends.

Although Ms. Martin left abruptly, do you predict that she will return during scheduled conferences to meet with Mr. Lindsay? Do you believe that she has faith in Mr. Lindsay's abilities as a teacher as well as his abilities in planning, organizing, and communicating?

## Keep in Mind

It should be noted that many small issues, particularly those that have occurred once, should be handled by the teacher. Although documentation of behavior is a must, a single incident does not always warrant a conference with a parent. This scenario depicted a teacher who attempted to pass judgment on a family, to redirect the parent in parenting style, and to show concern about a seven-year-old's future in social skills.

Obviously, no partnership was formed through this exchange of words between parent and teacher. How often does this occur? Although the purpose of conferencing is to promote partnerships between parents and teachers, often the conference may be scheduled when the teacher doesn't know what else to do.

As a result of this type of meeting, the parent often feels defensive, uncooperative, and "blamed" for the child's behavior. The parent may also feel that the teacher is unloading his/her responsibility, rather than handling a situation at school. It is in these difficult circumstances that teachers need to be properly prepared to effectively promote the feeling of "we-ness" with parents.

Another type of parent-teacher conference that involves difficult communication is an academic performance conference.

Almost all teachers encounter children who are not performing according to the teacher's (and/or school's) expectations. When this problem arises, most teachers feel an obligation to contact the parent before the regularly scheduled conference time (fall or spring). These conferences may be necessary to provide an advance warning of low grades, report cards with negative comments or markings, and/or to explain test scores that may be shared during the formal conference. The following chapter discusses academic conferences.

# Chapter 5

# ACADEMIC PERFORMANCE CONFERENCES

The purpose of schooling is to provide all children with equal opportunities for learning. The teacher's responsibility is to see that learning takes place. When young children experience failure in learning tasks, their self-concepts may be damaged, they may develop negative attitudes toward schooling, and they may be rejected by peers. As a result, parents may pressure children at home to improve performance. These are all difficult circumstances to consider in determining whether or not a child's academic performance is serious enough to initiate a parent-teacher conference.

It should be noted that conferences with parents concerning academic performance may be very positive meetings. Teachers who spend time with parents consulting about home studies, academic accomplishments and achievements (as opposed to problems/difficulties), and learning strengths, often reap the benefits of long-term positive alliances with parents. These conferences are also beneficial in establishing trust and rapport with parents. When interactions with parents are positive in nature, their attitudes toward school are generally more positive and supportive as a result.

The teacher's role in promoting learning for all children is a difficult task. When children experience difficulties, the teacher must be prepared to (1) find alternative learning/teaching strategies; (2) enlist the help of parents; and (3) continue to encourage the child so that the child feels good about him/herself.

When teachers determine that a child is not reaching the

expected academic performance level, they usually contact the parents. The primary purpose of this type of conference is to verbally report academic standing and to determine problem areas. It is most effective, however, to notify parents when the problem area arises rather than waiting until the traditional semiannual scheduled conferences occur. Meeting with parents to discuss grades and academic progress before the scheduled conferences accomplishes several goals:

- Parents feel included in the educational process.
- Parents are not surprised about academic standing when regularly scheduled conferences occur.
- Parents are provided opportunities for input in improving their child's performance.
- Parents help by working with the teacher and the child to improve learning.
- The link between home and school becomes stronger.

In determining whether a face-to-face meeting is necessary to discuss the academic performance of a child, the teacher must first choose a realistic area for improvement and set goals with the child. Conferencing with children has been found to be effective in improving academic performance (6, 53). Teachers may invest time interacting face-to-face with young children, setting goals, and working together toward those goals. Some children may thrive following this interaction and improvements may be measurable. A followup conference that could include both child and parent would then accomplish additional partnership goals.

## THREE-WAY CONFERENCES
## WITH PARENTS, CHILDREN, AND TEACHERS

In these three-way conferences, it is vital that all members perceive their specific input as valid and important. Although some may believe kindergartners and first graders are too young to take part in such conferences, these children may develop greater understanding of educational goals through their participation. A word of caution—throughout the conference, it is of utmost importance that no two parties develop an alliance against the third party; this can result in frustration, ambivalence, and/or feelings of inadequacy. The teacher's role is to facilitate discussion, promote partnerships among all participants, and encourage input for alternative plans of action.

There is a great deal of controversy concerning this type of meeting; many do not consider it appropriate in early childhood. This author supports the notion that three-way conferences may be beneficial when:

- The teacher determines that the child is mature and responsible enough to be included in the meeting.
- The child expresses interest in meeting with both parent and teacher.
- The parent agrees that a three-way conference would be helpful.
- Both parent and teacher are willing to listen open-mindedly to the child's input.
- The teacher considers him/herself to be competent in conferencing skills and may serve effectively as a facilitator.

The teacher's role in scheduling conferences is a very important one. It is a tremendous responsibility to make effective decisions concerning participation. Not only are the participants key factors in the effectiveness of the meeting, but also of importance are the agenda, the facilitation of discussion, and the development of collaboration among partners.

# CONFERENCING WITH PARENTS
# ABOUT ACADEMIC PERFORMANCE

When it is appropriate to contact the parent, caution and planning are in order. Parents must be enlisted as colleagues in the collaborative effort to educate children (29). When parents are asked to assume responsibilities for teacher-identified problems, teachers cannot hope to change the way in which parents view schools. This means that parents are asked for input, provided opportunities to state concerns and alternative solutions, and enlisted to work toward educating their children. When parents view the teacher as shifting responsibility from his/her shoulders to those of the parents, they become defensive, angry, and hostile.

As agents of the school, teachers should initiate conferences with parents and set the context of the meeting. Parents should be notified and provided a brief explanation as to the nature of the conference. Once again, a telephone conference is not as effective as face-to-face interaction, but a brief explanation of the purpose of the meeting is essential.

Because parents view their children as extensions of themselves, problem areas may be sensitive issues. Many parents experienced difficulties in school themselves; therefore, they may not express high expectations for their children in a specific subject area or, possibly, in all areas of schooling. On the other hand, some parents were high achievers and have unrealistic expectations for young children. It is necessary for teachers to determine the parents' expectation levels for their child before projecting additional expectations on the child (as well as the parent). The conference on academic performance may be used to cultivate partnerships that promote a better understanding of school goals, parental expectations, teacher expectations, and strategies for effective learning.

One helpful quality to cultivate is the ability to sense what parents want from you as a teacher. Whether parents articulate it or not, they would like to be assured that their child's teacher has the ability and willingness to view their child as an individual with intellectual, social, emotional, and physical strengths and weaknesses (36). "Parents appreciate a teacher who can make each learner feel 'special,' a teacher who gives warm assistance while insisting on each learner's academic growth and responsible behavior in the classroom" (36). Parents would like teachers to be aware of the current environment outside the school, past experiences, and events that may influence the child's behavior and performance in school. Once again, parents are an untapped resource in the education of young children. Their input and collaboration are invaluable to teachers. It is of utmost importance that they be included in the educational process. Through setting your own goals, you can assure parents that you are all they expect from a teacher.

In setting the tone for the meeting, the documentation, the arrangement of the environment, and the atmosphere established at the beginning of the conference are all key factors. An effective academic performance conference may follow the outlined steps of the Lawler Model. Although the agenda should not be too structured or too rigid to allow for parental interaction, there should be an agenda.

Once the conference has begun, the teacher should present as positively as possible the documented information regarding the particular area of concern. It is unwise to mislead or cover up unacceptable academic performance, but tact, poise, and self-assurance may assist in enlisting the help of parents. As previously noted, how one chooses to say what needs to be said has tremendous impact on how the other person receives the message (1).

Academic problems may create tension and uncertainty for parents. Avoid giving ultimatums, a "bottom line," and hopeless negative outcomes (such as grade retention). Such statements will cause parents to be overwhelmed, burdened, defensive, and angry. It should be pointed out that although academic learning is a major goal of schooling, parents, children, and teachers must work together to achieve this goal.

A conference should not become a power struggle. It is not a case of one person's dominance, but a serious meeting of the minds where everyone's point of view is equally considered. The teacher must exercise communication skills that are respectful. The content should be relevant, fairly brief, solution-oriented, and a stepping stone for future interactions with parents.

Academic performance conferences must include discussion of specific examples of work and objective observations of academic performance. Generalizations are not only inappropriate when discussing academics, but are frustrating and may erect communication barriers for parents. Problems affecting the child's performance must be dealt with directly (34). Only when the teacher is certain that accurate, specific messages have been sent and received may solutions be determined.

Paraphrasing and asking for clarification are important ingredients when conducting this type of conference. The teacher must make certain that the parent has heard the message as he/she intended it to be heard. The teacher must also provide plans for what he/she intends to do to intervene. A limited number of suggestions should be provided (1). Asking the parent for reactions to the alternative solutions (in the school setting) enables the parent to feel involved, valuable, and active.

Effective communication skills are necessary to assure that everyone is understanding the problem and is in agreement about outcomes and solutions. Asking such questions as, "Would you agree that . . . ?" and "How do you feel about . . . ?" enables the teacher to determine the parents' feelings, reactions, and input.

While listening to comments of parents, the teacher must hear the words and feelings behind the words (1). Some parents may be defensive because of personal feelings of inadequacy. Some may place blame on the teacher because of lack of knowledge about home study skills. Others may place blame on the child in unrealistic ways. Any reaction must be dealt with objectively, patiently, and open-mindedly.

Open-ended statements and reflective listening may assist in clarifying, alleviating misunderstandings, and preventing distrust. When parents feel that they are invited to comment and that their input is accepted, they are more positively responsive in collaborative efforts. They must also feel that the teacher is assuming some responsibility for the problem. When the teacher initiates comments about what he/she can do to contribute to solving the problem, the parents are more open-minded and willing to contribute as partners.

When making suggestions about home study habits, parental tutoring sessions, etc., speak in a clear tone and at a moderate pace. Parents must not feel that they are being treated in a condescending manner, or being ordered to engage in teacher-directed behaviors in their home. State suggestions as just that—suggestions.

After inviting the parents to contribute at home to the improvement of their child's academic performance, ask open-ended, clarifying questions to determine the parents' level of commitment and participation. Ask for the kind of help only a parent can give. Parents are often unaware of very simple home-life practices that may assist in the educational process— for example, providing encouragement, making sure the child has enough rest, keeping the child healthy, having a set study time, reading to the child (role modeling), monitoring TV watching, and staying in touch with the teacher. Once parents perceive that they are not only invited, but are encouraged, to initiate contact with the teacher, the school and the teacher may appear to be much less unapproachable to them than in the past.

Read the previously outlined conference vignette about Mark Bryan (see pp. 23–25). In the revised version that follows the teacher's role in the conference has been altered to promote a more effective meeting. Mrs. Carlson has telephoned Mrs.

Bryan to ask her to come in and discuss Mark's home study habits. This meeting is conducted before the regularly scheduled conference time.

## REVISED CONFERENCE VIGNETTE:
## MARK BRYAN*

MRS. CARLSON: Hello. I am Mrs. June Carlson, Mark's teacher. Are you Mrs. Bryan?

MRS. BRYAN: Yes. I am sorry to be late, Mrs. Carlson, but traffic was terrible.

MRS. CARLSON: That's understandable at this time of day, Mrs. Bryan, but please call me June. Mark tells me that you and Mr. Bryan are both attorneys. He seems very proud of you both.

MRS. BRYAN: Thank you for telling me that. I worry sometimes that we are both so busy that Mark may feel left out. It is hard to maintain a balance between work and home. Did you say there was a problem with Mark?

MRS. CARLSON: (You retrieve your file folder with Mark's work samples.) Well, Mrs. Bryan, Mark has performed beautifully in Reading and in Social Studies. He's been having difficulty lately in completing outside assignments and homework.

MRS. BRYAN: I had no idea that Mark had not completed his work at home. I have asked him several times lately, but he said that he didn't have homework. Just exactly what are the work assignments he left incomplete?

MRS. CARLSON: I have a few examples. One is a math pretest

---

*Adapted from "Simformation 6: Planning, Conducting, and Evaluating Parent-Teacher Conferences," by R. Cooper and others. National Institute of Education, Washington, D.C., 1977. ED 208 466.

that he failed to complete at home. Another is a reading comprehension worksheet given as homework last Thursday, and yesterday his report for Science on "Crocodiles" was incomplete. He turned in a draft, but was to rewrite it at home according to my suggestions and recommendations, and return it yesterday. When I questioned him about it he said that he doesn't have a place to study at home where he can put out his materials and work quietly. (You pause.)

MRS. BRYAN: Well, I suppose he's right. My husband and I use the study and the dining room table to work on cases in the evenings. Mark's bedroom does not have a desk or table, so I guess he feels as though he needs a work space of his own.

MRS. CARLSON: Mrs. Bryan, I wanted to talk to you about this now before it became a more serious problem. Mark is usually very conscientious and turns in quality work. He is very bright. I was just interested in talking with you about how we could help Mark finish all his assignments.

MRS. BRYAN: I am glad you called, Mrs. Carlson. We would like Mark to go on to law school. My husband graduated from Yale, you know. We know that it takes hard work and a high grade point average to be accepted into law school. We wouldn't want Mark to fall behind.

MRS. CARLSON: Mark has assured me that he will try to do better, but I felt that talking with you about it in person would be helpful. Could we talk about some things that both of us could do to improve Mark's work habits at home?

MRS. BRYAN: I'm not sure you can do anything. I'll have to talk with Mark about this and try to find a place for him to study. His father will not be happy about this.

MRS. CARLSON: Maybe I could help Mark make a list of his homework assignments and put it in a folder along with the work. When he comes home, you might look at the folder and see what he is supposed to complete. I'm not sure about where Mark could work, but I'll be happy to keep you up to date on his progress.

MRS. BRYAN: The folder sounds good. Maybe the kitchen table would be quiet and spacious enough for him to work and feel as though he has a place of his own.

MRS. CARLSON: That sounds like a good idea. Would you like to schedule another meeting with me in, say, two weeks, or would you like me to give you a call and see if we need an additional meeting?

MRS. BRYAN: I would appreciate the phone call. His father and I want him to do well in school. If I need to come in again soon, I will schedule a time with you. Thank you for talking to me about this. Are there other problems with Mark?

MRS. CARLSON: I believe that the most important issue, now, is for us to help Mark finish work at home. I believe that Mark can successfully complete all the work, but I do assign grades and I would not want him to receive a poor grade on his report card due to incomplete work.

MRS. BRYAN: I don't believe that you said whether there was another problem that we needed to discuss.

MRS. CARLSON: No. I don't think we need to discuss anything else at this time. Mark is doing well in other subjects and has not been a behavior problem. I appreciate your concern and your time. Please let me know if there is anything else I can do to help here at school.

MRS. BRYAN: Thank you, June. I will see you soon, but I hope we both have good things to say. (She leaves.)

## REVIEW OF THE MARK BRYAN CONFERENCE AND THE LAWLER MODEL

The conference was brief, to the point, and appeared to

be successful. Mrs. Carlson's attitude was very different from her attitude in the earlier conference. Mrs. Carlson was not defensive, did not make general negative or derogatory comments about her class, and did not make accusatory remarks to Mrs. Bryan. Mrs. Carlson was open-minded, nonjudgmental, and expressed interest in obtaining Mrs. Bryan's help.

Mrs. Bryan was interested, concerned, and offered suggestions for changes she could make at home. She did not accuse Mrs. Carlson or jump to conclusions.

Look at the conference sequence with reference to the Lawler Model:

> L—LOCATE. Mrs. Carlson had collected specific examples to demonstrate Mark's lack of productivity at home. She was well organized, she provided documentation, and she was brief. She did not overwhelm the parent. She had also briefed Mrs. Bryan on Mark's problem.

> A—ARRANGE THE ENVIRONMENT. The meeting appeared to take place in a relaxed, comfortable atmosphere. Mrs. Bryan did not mention being uncomfortable, nor did she sound defensive. Mrs. Carlson had checked school records to determine Mrs. Bryan's preferred last name. She called her by name and made her feel welcome.

> W—WORK TOWARD PARTNERSHIPS. Mrs. Carlson began on a positive note. First, she established rapport with Mrs. Bryan. She asked for input from Mrs. Bryan and reiterated what she had said. They discussed educational plans. Although Mrs. Carlson did not offer more than one alternative, her suggestion was well received by Mrs. Bryan.

> L—LISTEN. Mrs. Carlson listened and responded to Mrs. Bryan's questions, comments, and suggestions.

E—EVALUATE. Mrs. Carlson appeared to evaluate as the conference progressed. It was evident from her comments that she was very attentive, she attempted to be empathetic with Mrs. Bryan, and she was supportive of Mrs. Bryan's suggestions.

R—RESPOND. Mrs. Carlson responded well to Mrs. Bryan. She asked Mrs. Bryan for suggestions regarding followup plans. The meeting appeared to end on a positive note. Mrs. Bryan seemed to be encouraged and positive about Mrs. Carlson and helping Mark become more productive. She did not seem to be defensive, angry, or intimidated.

Although Mrs. Carlson did not respond appropriately about additional problems (she avoided discussing behavior), she did very well in discussing and arriving at solutions to the academic performance problem. She should have indicated that there had been minor behavior problems lately but they had worked them out. She could have continued a step further by assuring Mrs. Bryan that if a behavior problem recurred or escalated, she would contact her.

Mrs. Carlson did not want to address more than one issue in the conference (and rightfully so), but she should not skirt or blur issues. Parents may be offended, feel that information is being withheld, and possibly become angry.

One of the most difficult interactions that occurs between teachers and parents is the conference in which referrals are made concerning learning disabilities and other handicapping conditions. The following chapter discusses these conferences and provides recommendations for making them effective meetings.

# Chapter 6

# REFERRAL CONFERENCES

Parent involvement became a significant factor in public education with the funding of such federal programs as Head Start, Follow Through, and Title I (51). The federal government's role in parent involvement became more direct with the enactment of Public Law 93-390. This law served the major purpose of protecting the educational rights established in the Rehabilitation Act of 1973 (60). The Buckley Amendment to Public Law 93-390 protects the rights and privacy of all students and parents. It states that schools cannot release information or a child's records without parental consent. The amendment establishes parents' right of access to their children's school records and their right to challenge information in the records that they deem inaccurate or inappropriate.

PL 94-142, passed in 1975, specifically requires the direct participation of parents, teachers, and, when appropriate, the exceptional child in the Individualized Education Program (IEP). This law has enabled parents to participate in evaluation procedures; challenge the appropriateness of placement or program; assist in planning educational goals and objectives; have access to school records; and attend public hearings on state special education decisions. The IEP provision of PL 94-142 requires that parents and educators cooperatively develop and provide educational and related services in response to the needs of each exceptional child.

These meetings appear to be dreaded by teachers. This dread seems somewhat warranted in light of teachers' lack of preparation and training in the necessary skills for effectively conducting these meetings. In a survey of undergraduate students, Price discovered that conducting parent-teacher conferences was considered one of the most anxiety-provoking aspects of their future jobs: "Concern about these hearings and various other forms of legal action may contribute significantly to teachers' anxiety in communicating with parents" (52).

Although society is becoming increasingly aware of the needs of exceptional children, "parents of handicapped children are still faced with inadequate understanding and a society that is greatly intolerant of deviations from the norm" (20). And although the *role* of parenting encountered by parents of handicapped individuals is similar to that of parents of nonhandicapped children, many times they encounter *conditions* and situations that parents of nonhandicapped children may never experience. As Gargiulo observes, "It is important to remember that a handicapped child is first and foremost a child" (20). Parents of these children are first and foremost parents. They often need assistance in facing and sorting out their emotional reactions. As educators, our role is to help parents make this adjustment as smoothly and painlessly as possible.

Gargiulo further observes:

> Parents have often represented an untapped resource for professionals who work with exceptional children. Inasmuch as parents are capable of making valuable contributions, their involvement with professionals is important to the development of the handicapped person. In comparison with professionals, parents have a greater investment in their children, not only of time but also of emotion. No other person will know the child as well as the parents do. Their experiences predate and exceed those of any professional. As a consequence, they have more influence and are capable of assuming a more positive and active role than traditionally accorded to them. (20)

In other words, the bad old days are gone. "Parents of children with disabilities no longer are ignored" (21). In a recent national study, various groups of professionals ranked parent involvement as one of the top five educational priority areas.

Although this was ranked a priority, the major question and concern of educators should be the communication between parents and teachers. The role of the teacher is that of facilitator, guide, supporter, and partner in making educational decisions concerning a handicapped child.

As Faerstein points out, usually it is not until the child reaches school age that a diagnosis of a learning disorder is made (16). Consequently, it is frequently the role of the teacher and other educational professionals to first discuss the possibility of the existence of a handicapping condition with the child's parents (57). Being the bearer of such unhappy news is a very difficult task; teachers should take into account the coping mechanisms and emotions that come into play when parents are confronted with the issue of their child's disability. The teacher's role is to provide parents with precise, easily understandable information about the child's skill levels. When all options for student learning have been exhausted, the teacher must suggest to the child's parent that an evaluation outside the classroom be made. "It is reasonable to assume that by the time a parent-teacher conference has been scheduled to discuss a possible learning disability, the parent has sensed for a while that something is amiss, even though it has remained unspoken" (57).

## PARENTAL REACTIONS TO HANDICAPPING CONDITIONS

Faerstein contended that the parents' defense mechanism of denial is most likely to have developed by the time of the prediagnosis conference (15). A child with a possible learning disability may have demonstrated academic ability in some areas, leading the parents to believe that more "effort" would improve the child's achievement in other areas. At previous conferences the parents may have attributed the child's lack of achievement in specific learning areas to laziness or uncooperativeness. They may have made this inappropriate diagnosis because of their lack of understanding of the nature of learning disabilities. If the lack of performance were due to specified characteristics such as laziness or uncooperativeness, it would seen to be controllable. Admission and acceptance of news about any type of handicapping condition, in the parents' eyes, are often the admission of defeat and surrender.

Although parents may react in a variety of ways and may experience emotional reactions in stages, it should be noted that these reactions are natural, legitimate, automatic, understandable, and normal (20). During this type of conference the parent may react in some of the ways outlined below, but it is most likely that these emotional responses will occur during or following the interdisciplinary assessment team meeting. When teachers approach parents about testing for diagnosis of a learning difficulty, many parents (emotionally) deny that any problem exists. They agree in order to confirm their suspicions; they are in the denial phase.

Parents do appear to experience stages of reactions to handicapping conditions. Their reactions may not follow a sequential pattern; some may never progress beyond hurt and anger. In some cases, "this may be their initial exposure to a disability label" (20).

Generally, psychologists and educators of handicapped individuals have reached consensus on three phases of parental emotional reactions to handicapping conditions: primary, secondary, and tertiary. Gargiulo (20) further described the levels within each phase as detailed below.

*Primary Phase*

1. *Shock.* This may be characterized by symptoms of irrational behavior, excessive crying, feelings of numbness and helplessness.
2. *Denial.* Parents may refuse to recognize the child's deficiency and may attempt to rationalize atypical behaviors of the child. Their reactions may also be

more subtle by becoming too cooperative with professionals. When this occurs, parents agree to any suggestions/recommendations outlined on the Individualized Education Program (IEP), but later question and challenge the IEP content.

3. *Grief and depression.* Most parents are typically disappointed about handicapping conditions and are realistically concerned about coping with the handicapped child.

## Secondary Phase

4. *Ambivalence.* "A child with disabilities is capable of intensifying the normal emotions of love and anger experienced by most parents toward their child" (20). Parents may even reject the child as well as the reality that the child possesses a handicapping condition.

5. *Guilt.* This is one of the most difficult reactions to overcome. During this phase, overcompensation is common. Parents may try to "make it up" to the child. The handicap may become more important than the child.

6. *Anger.* This type of anger is usually expressed in two ways. The first type is often expressed in fairness and question—"Why me?" The second type may be expressed through rage directed at others.

7. *Shame and embarrassment.* Many times parents of handicapped children learn to anticipate social rejection, pity, and ridicule of society in general.

## Tertiary Phase

8. *Bargaining.* This is one of the final stages of adjustment. Parents hope to "bargain" with God, science, or anyone who may make their child normal.

9. *Adaptation and reorganization.* This level consists of a gradual process requiring varying lengths of time and

a reduction in feelings of anxiety as well as other emotional reactions. During this phase parents increase their abilities to deal with their responsibility for the child's problems.

10. *Acceptance and adjustment.* "Acceptance is the goal that most parents strive for" (20). To adjust and accept the handicapping condition, parents must exhibit conscious efforts to recognize, understand, and resolve problems.

In order that teachers may work cooperatively and communicate effectively with parents concerning children with various handicapping conditions, awareness and acceptance of these phases are important. Teachers must be willing to listen carefully and nonjudgmentally to parental anxieties, concerns, and frustrations with their young children. Greater willingness to listen, to accept, and to cooperate are necessary if teachers are to develop partnerships with parents of these special children.

Referrals are often the most anxiety-provoking conferences in which teachers participate. Many teachers are inexperienced in communicating about these critical problems; there is a significant (and often costly) decision to be made concerning the child's welfare. When meeting with a parent regarding initial services that could be provided through PL 94-142, the teacher should consider information about the child's progress and social/emotional behaviors, and be aware of parental reactions.

These conferences are usually conducted within the same framework as regularly scheduled conferences and may follow the Lawler Model. It should be noted, however, that establishing a partnership with these parents concerning additional services to be provided their child is one of the most important relationships to be established within the teaching realm. The initial conference marks the beginning of a cooperative working relationship between the parents and the professionals in providing educational services for the child. Only when parental cooperation, support, and acceptance are evident does the process becomes a partnership.

When parents are uncooperative and defensive about initial testing and referral processes, the teacher can review the parental reaction phases outlined above and respond to the parents accordingly.

Rather than giving up hope when parental reactions are negative, it is most effective to continue interacting with parents; to accept their feelings, allowing time for their reactions to progress through the various phases; and to work positively toward partnerships. If a parent refuses to permit the assessment procedures, be supportive, accepting, and give the parent time for emotional reaction.

After allowing time for reactions, contact the parent again and discuss the assessment procedures a second time. On a more positive note, sometimes after thoughtful consideration, the parent may contact the teacher to discuss proceeding with assessment. Remember, most parents want what is best for their children. They view them as extensions of themselves. They do not purposely deny them appropriate education, even though they are sometimes hurt, angry, and frustrated by problems in the educational process. As Gargiulo makes clear, parents may feel guilty and/or consider themselves failures because of their child's academic performance (20).

One major difference between this type of conference and a regularly scheduled meeting with parents is that the followup conference is mandated. After the testing procedures, PL 94-142 requires that the parent(s) attend the IEP meeting and serve as participant(s) with the interdisciplinary assessment team. The followup meeting is usually conducted in a setting other than the regular classroom; several professionals attend to give information and further explanation about the services to be provided.

# INTERDISCIPLINARY ASSESSMENT TEAM MEETINGS

PL 94-142 changed the status of parents from mere recipients to active participants in the education of their children. It "ushered in a new era in parent-professional interaction," since "the IEP process requires that educators and parents formulate decisions in a cooperative manner" (20).

Under the provisions of PL 94-142, the legal and civil rights of each handicapped child are protected by due process procedures. There is protection in evaluation procedures to ensure that tests administered to determine placement are valid and are given in the child's native language. Following the assessment, an individualized education program (IEP) must be prepared. It must include "a statement of the objectives, a description of the services to be provided, and an explanation of the criteria to be used for determining achievement of objectives" (4). The IEP is prepared by the members of the interdisciplinary assessment team, the classroom teacher, and the parents of the child.

Fiscus and Mandell identified the six stages of the IEP process in which parents and professionals work together in shared responsibilities:

- information gathering
- decision making
- identification and assessment
- placement and program planning
- program implementation
- program monitoring and evaluation. (17)

The process requires that educators and parents formulate decisions in a cooperative manner (20). Most cooperative relationships between parents and professionals develop into partnerships. The question to ask is, "What kind of partnership can be established?" It is the responsibility of professionals to establish cooperative working relationships with parents of handicapped children by trying to understand them, their emotions, and their needs. These skills may be developed only through effective communication.

The interdisciplinary assessment team may consist of psychologists, counselor, the school district's authorized assessment specialist, and others, including the building principal, who may be involved in determining the services to be provided. It should be noted that the parents are a part of this team, are members in the planning phase, and, according to the legal and civil rights stated in PL 94-142, are to assist in writing the IEP. This is important to note because in many cases parents are included in a meeting conducted after the IEP is written and are *not* asked for input, but for a signature of approval. The IEP is a team effort, legally mandated by PL 94-142, designed to involve the parents and to acquire their knowledge and input while determining what specific services may be provided to their child.

It has been reported that many times parents feel threatened and intimidated by this group meeting (4, 17, 20). It has also been reported that although parents may spend a moderate amount of time responding and initiating comments during these meetings, they spend very little time asking questions (63). Vaughn, Bos, Harrell, and Lasky gave the following possible reasons for lack of parental questions: (1) parents may feel comfortable with their level of participation and be satisfied that questions will be answered throughout the meeting; (2) parental knowledge of their child's handicapping condition is not great enough for them to participate more fully; (3) personnel perceive the parental role as passive/listener in the meeting; and (4) a mismatch exists between the communication pattern established prior to the conference (one-to-one communication with the classroom teacher) and the pattern established during the meeting (three to five professionals discussing with one to two parents (63).

Parents attend the meeting and are in the school setting (a somewhat foreign environment), discussing an educational decision concerning their child with professionals who appear confident, prepared, and knowledgeable. Psychologically, parents feel threatened merely by the ratio of parents and professionals. They perceive that they are being pressured simply because there are more people attending the meeting who work with the child in the school setting than in the home environment. The professionals attending the meeting often perform systematically and routinely. This further intimidates parents in that they feel as if they are the only team members unfamiliar with the terminologies and procedures. Unfortunately, they are often correct in this perception. Professionals must be aware of terminologies, the emotional reactions to the conference environment, and group status.

During this phase of the educational process (IEP meeting), parental reactions may occur. Although parents may not begin to exhibit the emotional reaction behaviors previously outlined, they may experience them within, and internalize them temporarily. Following this interdisciplinary assessment team meeting, the parents may return for a visit and exhibit some of the emotional reactions that are normal, understandable, and legitimate.

A most important guideline for the classroom teacher is to determine the local ground rules in referral and IEP meetings (4). It is almost certain that classroom teachers will be involved in the IEP meeting and will also be involved with the team members conducting the assessment as well as those providing the special services. The parents will also be involved in the process and may be asked to support the efforts through activities and tasks conducted with the child at home. The classroom teacher may be asked by the parent for clarification, further instructions, and support, particularly since the parent will be more familiar with the classroom teacher than with any other team member. The classroom teacher's role is that of instructor to the child within

70

the regular classroom setting, guide and supporter of parents, team member on the interdisciplinary assessment team, and coauthor in the IEP process.

The key to successful IEP meetings is for parents to become active participants in establishing the goals and objectives for accomplishment. The child's education will be provided by the professionals who serve the special needs of the child, the classroom teacher who will provide regular service and who will support the resource personnel, and the parents who will support both professionals (resource and classroom teacher) through home educational activities. Parents will also serve as facilitators and supporters of the child in his/her learning efforts. An active role played by the parent will promote successful outcomes for the child who has special needs.

The following chapter discusses types of conferences that are not within the realm of scheduled parent-teacher conferences. Many of the circumstances discussed include conflicts.

# Chapter 7

# CONFERENCES ABOUT DISCIPLINE PROBLEMS

When problems arise from the teacher's perspective and parents must be contacted, the problems must be handled delicately, diplomatically, objectively, and in a somewhat relaxed, personable manner. These conferences are often viewed as monsters hovering on the school calendar to prevent teachers from enjoying their week. Discipline conferences may not always be enjoyable, but they may produce satisfactory results for everyone involved when they are conducted effectively.

Discipline conferences should be viewed as opportunities (29). Parents and teachers establish rapport and trust through meetings when there are no apparent problems. Meetings between parents and teachers are more productive and effective then when they attempt to solve problems together. Particularly in discipline situations, it is important to consult with parents. Parents have insights into their child's behavior patterns, past experiences, social relationships, social and emotional insecurities, and many other influential factors. These insights may assist in producing solutions to school-related problems. As Hayes puts it, "Too often teachers approach these conferences as if parents and their children have a problem for which the teacher is somehow responsible" (29). This attitude can only lead to no-win discussions, more problems among parents, children, and teacher, as well as the destruction of any previous partnership established between the teacher and the particular parent.

Although discipline conferences may not follow the Lawler Model explicitly, the steps and procedures may be helpful. Teachers must collect accurate information to share with parents regarding specific behavior incidents. They must also arrange the environment for an effective conference. Even in difficult interactions with parents, a partnership remains the primary goal.

Without parents as partners, some problem situations may never be resolved. When parents are aware of this need, their reactions are generally much more positive, open, and cooperative. It is crucial that the teacher listen openly and reflectively, and respond to parents' concerns, suggestions, and recommendations. The conference may be evaluated as it proceeds and a followup will be necessary—either written or verbal.

In these ways, the discipline conference may proceed very similarly to the scheduled conferences previously discussed. The nature of the conference may be different, but the goals and objectives are the same—parents should have input, they should become more aware of school events, and they should work as partners with teachers in educating young children.

When discipline problems arise, the teacher must first determine who owns the problem. As in the case of Sujette, many times the teacher's reaction may create a problem situation. Many discipline problems may be solved within the classroom between the teacher and the child. Often it is best to consider the behavior, the motive behind the behavior, and possible solutions, and attempt to work it out with the child first. If, after attempting to work with the child toward a common goal (improved behavior), positive outcomes are not reached, contacting the parent is the appropriate alternative.

However, teachers should not wait to contact the parent until frustrations have mounted with the child. At this point they come across negatively to the parent. Sending notes (one-way communication) to inform parents of an initial discipline problem is, unfortunately, ineffective. Parents often feel intimidated by teachers, their written communication, and especially the negative report about the child. It is more effective to telephone, briefly explain some of the problem (so that the parent is not in the dark), and ask the parent to come in to discuss the situation. Parents may then collect their thoughts, form questions, and possibly determine alternative solutions before meeting face-to-face with the teacher.

If parents cannot be reached by telephone and the teacher considers the problem important enough to discuss with them, then a note requesting a meeting is appropriate. The note should, however, include a brief explanation of the nature of the meeting and give the parents an opportunity for input about the time and place of the meeting. Once these factors have been determined, the meeting may begin more effectively.

Because teachers are in the unique position of working with so many children in one age group, they may recognize atypical behavior long before the parents do (8). The sooner a problem is detected and help is obtained, the more likely it is that a change will occur. But teachers must first determine who owns the problem—the teacher or the child. If, indeed, the child's behavior is the problem, not the teacher's reaction to the behavior, then the parent should be contacted as soon as possible.

One caution—discipline conferences should not be used as vendettas against children who have been particular nuisances. The objective of these conferences should not be to settle any score. The teacher's role is that of partner of children and parents to improve learning. When discipline problems arise, the essential problem is that maximum learning may not occur in the classroom. With this thought in mind, the objective of alternative solutions to such problems should be to promote maximum learning, not to damage self-concepts or change parental style.

Parents who feel good about themselves are better equipped to provide their children with the encouragement needed to resolve a problem. As Morgan expresses it, "The values and experiences of parents, teachers, and administrators are strong influences on their definitions of problem behaviors and appropriate guidance techniques" (47). Educational, religious, familial, socioeconomic, and cultural backgrounds can all influence perceptions of problems and choice of discipline

75

methods; "additionally, stress (e.g., marital, medical, financial) can influence parents' perception of a problem" (19).

Teachers have an obligation to inform parents when problem behaviors exist. If partnerships are to be created, they must be established by working cooperatively with parents in problem-solving situations. Keeping the child's welfare central and conveying mutuality of interest should be the conference priority (22). Remember to handle the meeting in a straightforward and honest manner, explaining your objective and requesting input from the parent. If a parent sees you as blaming and attacking, he/she may become defensive and stop listening.

It is best not to unload too much on the parent at one time (8). It is also important to clearly describe the particular concern by painting a picture of the specific events or actions so that the parents can see the problem behavior from your perspective.

Barron and Colvin advise that "choice of words is of utmost importance when discussing a problem" (1). Once a realistic area of student behavior has been identified for improvement, present the problem to the parent in a nonaccusatory manner. Be specific and provide objective descriptions of occurrences. Parents must not feel as if the teacher is speaking to them in a condescending manner. And overdiscussion of the problem behavior is nonproductive (52).

Avoid mentioning other children or parents. To maintain confidentiality among teachers, parents, and children, it is important that each child, her or his individual behavior patterns, and resulting solutions to problem areas be discussed only between the involved parents, the child, and the teacher. If parents try to interject comparisons or quote other parents, firmly and quickly refer to the immediate situation and the specific child being discussed. How we say what we say has a tremendous impact on how the other person receives the message (1). Words like "seem, appear, perhaps, and maybe" are tentative and less final than "is, should, and always" (1). To prevent parental alienation, avoid such phrases as "We think you should . . . " and "You can't hold us responsible . . ." (34).

The teacher is chiefly in control of the discipline conference, but this control means that the teacher does not dominate the conversation and allows the parent to express his or her feelings. "Control" means that the teacher is always aware that he or she is responsible for seeing that the conference moves toward a specific goal (45).

Sincere interest and honed listening skills will provide teachers with tools for effective outcomes. Listen carefully to parents' reactions and suggestions, and they will participate more openly. Allow parents to talk about their concerns without interruption rather than attempting to clarify or justify while they speak. "Be observant and recognize that the conference is a two-way experience" (22). Pay attention to behaviors of parents. Look for signs of fatigue, anxiety, restlessness, fear, or anger.

It is important to seek collaboration rather than cooperation. Cooperation too often means that one person goes along with but remains uncommitted to a plan of another. Collaboration requires working together to identify mutual concerns and to develop goals and a means to an end (29). "Collaboration is an interdependent relationship that places special demands on people to share their resources in a trusting relationship" (29). To facilitate collaboration, teachers must also be willing to assume some responsibility for the problem. It is evident that a problem exists or the discipline conference would not be scheduled. If the teacher can assume some responsibility for the resulting outcomes, however, the collaborative efforts may emerge.

Try to reach closure only after the parent has apparently finished giving reactions and suggestions. Summarizing the conference enables teacher and parent to check for mutual understanding of alternatives and future plans. Followup plans should be arranged when necessary. Most discipline conferences require a followup visit. It is most effective to maintain the partnership while alleviating discipline problems. When parent and teacher agree that a followup conference is unnecessary, a written note, a phone call, or other form of communication is appropriate.

The vignette in Appendix B supplies an example of a discipline conference. Put yourself in the role of the teacher, Mrs. Center, and think about ways the communication process could be improved.

Although discipline and other problem conferences that occur during times other than the semiannual scheduled conferences will vary, the format should be similar to that of regularly scheduled conferences. The Lawler Model may not be used in its entirety, but it may serve as a guide in planning all conferences with parents. The teacher is in control of the meeting and therefore has the responsibility for seeing that it is effective and productive, and that the partnership is established, enhanced, and maintained. This is a tremendous responsibility, especially when conflicts arise. Effective communication skills are essential throughout these difficult meetings.

When conflicts arise, teachers are often put on the spot. Discipline conferences and academic problem conferences may seem to be possible platforms for conflicts between parents and teachers. The following chapter discusses such conflicts and possible alternative ways to manage and/or resolve them.

# Chapter 8

# CONFLICTS BETWEEN PARENTS AND TEACHERS

Parents and teachers will not always agree on practices, beliefs, and/or procedures in the educational process. But it is important that they reach consensus and accept each other's thoughts, beliefs, and opinions.

All conferences are different. No two conferences are alike. Because children are unique individuals and parents respond to teachers in different ways, conferencing is an individualized process. Human relations skills are important in relating to each person individually. To develop positive relationships between home and school, teachers must maintain an attitude of openness and acceptance toward parents and children. An attitude that encourages parents to communicate with teachers concerning positive and negative aspects of schooling is also essential.

Teachers usually experience anxieties when meeting with parents for the first time. When delicate issues arise, they often fear the worst possible reactions from parents. On the other hand, parents often suffer anxieties and uncertainties when asked to meet with teachers for the first time. Negative connotations regarding conferences derive from a consensus that meetings with teachers are most likely scheduled to discuss problems. Parents experience dread before meeting face-to-face with teachers to discuss problems. What can help remedy these fears, anxieties, and uncertainties?

The best public relations strategy for teachers to use in parental involvement is frequent communication with parents concerning positive circumstances and accomplishments of their children. Communicating with parents, even in one-way forms, when things are running smoothly and positive things are happening suggests an investment of interest between both teacher and parent. A relationship develops through these positive interactions; therefore, when problems need to be resolved, the rapport and trust previously established may provide a foundation on which to build.

When problems do arise, teachers must first establish rapport and trust with parents through telephone discussion. Alerting the parent that a problem exists and briefly explaining the necessity for face-to-face interaction is essential. Most parents express a greater fear of the unknown than of dealing directly with an identified problem.

After initiating telephone contact and arranging a meeting, it is important that the teacher lessen the parent's initial anxiety and negative feelings (13). The teacher's ability to help the parent depends partly on conveying a sense of confidence in him/herself without appearing arrogant. When parents feel that school personnel are unsympathetic or arrogant, they may adopt an overbearing stance and may become irate (13). Sincere interest and empathetic understanding can indicate respect for the parent. The teacher must convey the message that helping the child develop as a person and as a student is the ultimate goal of the conference.

Different parents require different approaches. As Ellenburg and Lanier observe, "some parents are able to respond constructively and quickly when provided with appropriate information about their children's difficulties and the resources available to help them" (13). Unfortunately, many teachers fall into the trap of *assuming* that all parents respond to this approach. It is critical that teachers establish rapport and trust, and develop an understanding of the parent's style. This can lead to greater success in solving problems cooperatively with parents.

Ellenburg and Lanier also warn that "in trying to cope with a problem, parents sometimes blame teachers for not teaching their child appropriately or not giving them enough individualized attention" (13). In such cases, it is important to demystify the teacher's authority (29). It is also essential that the teacher be prepared to say something positive about the child. Parents are more likely to work toward something they can believe in than something that seems hopeless (29).

If the parents have not mentioned it, ask if they see certain behavior patterns at home. If they reply in the negative, accept their word and do not try to convince them otherwise (13). Teachers have nothing to gain by arguing, promoting their own perceptions, or attempting to convince parents that they are "wrong." Explain that children sometimes behave very differently at home and at school, and that they sometimes behave differently with different people. Be sure that parents are understanding exactly what you are trying to say. Avoid words like "can't" and "never." Ask for suggestions and use wait time for parents' answers. Wait time may be five to seven seconds; try not to make parents feel uncomfortable in the interim. A certain amount of thinking time is necessary to solve problems. Allow parents the opportunity to react and ventilate. Listen very actively and attentively to them. Discuss the problem in terms of how it might affect the child's immediate future if it continues. Do *not* make predictions or offer ultimatums. Such statements do not promote collaborative efforts or partnerships.

Parents, when upset, may use defense mechanisms. Such reactions "provide a means by which human beings can cope with pressures" (13). Parental defenses may vary from sweet, manipulating personalities to a rationalization that the teacher is the primary reason for the child's failure. When parents are ready to accept the information, to provide input regarding a solution to the problem, and to view the teacher as nonjudgmental and helpful, the problem may be solved. Remember, above all, to treat parents with dignity; convey a sense of acceptance (13).

Fuery recommended the value of apologizing: "Upset parents usually revert back to calm and collected people once they hear all the facts, and if an apology is in order, make the effort. We all make mistakes" (18).

When parents appear to be receptive, develop a plan of action, solicit help from them, and plan for followup. Action at the critical time is a key ingredient to conflict resolution. When parents exhibit cooperative and responsive attitudes, act quickly.

Swick and Duff recommended that teachers develop four behaviors to work effectively toward solving conflicts:

- Approachability—The teacher exhibits willingness to listen to the ideas of the parent.
- Flexibility—The teacher is adaptable to the needs of others.
- Sensitivity—The teacher treats each parent as an important human being.
- Dependability—The teacher usually gains a positive image in the eyes of the parent. (62)

It is beneficial for teachers to possess and cultivate these traits. Parents will respond more positively to teachers they perceive to be approachable, flexible, sensitive, and dependable.

The following parent-teacher exchange illustrates how teachers may foster parental support without blame.

## INTERACTION WITHOUT BLAME*

TEACHER: I would like to share my concerns about Preston's behavior at school. He does well in his academic work, but during class time he calls out answers, makes fun of his friends when they make errors, and teases children to the point that a physical confrontation often occurs. I talked with Preston about this, but he blamed his peers. He did finally admit that he behaved badly. He has said that he will try to improve his behavior.

---

*Adapted from "Conferencing Skills: Working with Parents," by E.M. Reiss, *Clearing House* 62, no. 2 (October 1988): 81-83.

MOTHER: I'm sorry. He knows better than that. I thought that Preston told me that he had to stay after school a few days. He has been taught to be good at school.

FATHER: I don't like it either. He knows that when he gets in trouble at school he also gets in trouble at home.

MOTHER: I don't know what *we* can do to control his behavior at school. We don't really have a problem with him at home.

FATHER: That's true. We tell him to do what we want him to and if he doesn't, he gets a spanking.

TEACHER: I share your frustration about this problem. I know that you are hearing this for the first time. With help from both of you, and from Preston, we can work out a plan, I'm sure. Let me tell you some of the alternatives that Preston and I have already tried.

MOTHER: You mentioned working out a plan with Preston. I'm confused.

FATHER: I don't want Preston in on our discussions.

TEACHER: Can you tell me more about why you feel uncomfortable involving Preston in our discussions?

FATHER: Well, I'm not uncomfortable, exactly. I just think we should have our act together before we include him in the process.

MOTHER: Maybe if we talk to him together, he will know that we all want to help.

TEACHER: I think that you are right about us discussing some alternatives first. Let's talk about what we can do to help Preston control himself during class time.

This exchange indicates that the teacher is acting as facilitator and allowing for input from parents. The teacher is persistent in her conviction that Preston should be included in the conference.

She does appear to be relatively diplomatic and encouraging with the parents. The parents have remained calm and appear receptive to working out the problem. This is the ultimate goal in conflict resolution and problem conferencing—reaching mutually acceptable agreements to work toward common goals.

Conflicts should be handled professionally and in a manner that fosters collaborative relationships rather than hard feelings, negative attitudes of parents toward school, and/or defensive reactions to the problem itself (55).

# Chapter 9

# CONFERENCES THAT GO AMISS AND CONFERENCES WITHOUT AGENDAS

## CONFERENCES THAT GO AMISS

Not every conference will proceed as planned. Some conferences may be conducted using the steps of the Lawler Model and the followup conferences may proceed even more smoothly than the previous meeting. Many times, however, parents come to the meeting with a conflicting agenda (see Appendix C). The teacher's agenda may also deviate from the original plan.

All teachers will confront an irate parent from time to time. Sometimes early in the meeting parents express hostilities and this cannot be avoided. Provided that parents are not abusive, it is better to allow them the opportunity to ventilate and express their feelings. This gives the teacher time to think. When the anger is directed toward a classroom situation or school-related issue, take notes and offer to discuss this with parents *after* investigating the issue. If the anger is directed toward the teacher personally, consider adding a third party (preferably the principal), or moving the conference to the principal's office. If possible, turn the discussion around by diplomatically suggesting that you (the teacher) would be happy to discuss this "issue" with them at another meeting, but that you would like to spend *this* designated time talking about their child, as you had previously arranged to do. If the parents do not accept this suggestion and insist on continuing the criticism or abuse, end the conference firmly but courteously.

# CONFERENCES WITHOUT AGENDAS

Many impromptu meetings are likely to occur between parents and teachers. Parents often arrive at a teacher's classroom without previously arranging the meeting. They may also show up immediately before or after school to discuss a problem. Sometimes parents ask to meet with teachers to discuss concerns. On such occasions, no one can be completely prepared, but there are steps to take that will better prepare you for these surprise visits.

Morgan suggested that teachers keep these points in mind when parents express concerns:

- Parents have a strong emotional investment in their children.
- A parent may actually be asking, "Am I a good parent?"
- Parents' definitions of normal and acceptable behavior are influenced by their understanding of typical growth and development of young children.
- The value and experiences of parents, teachers, and administrators are strong influences on their definitions of problem behaviors and appropriate guidance techniques.
- Teachers do not have to give immediate answers to parents' questions. (47)

One mistake teachers commonly make when parents initiate conferences is to perceive an obligation to provide immediate explanations, suggestions, and/or answers. Many times, parents want to use the teacher as a sounding board. They may need a sympathetic ear to hear problems, concerns, and frustrations. Although teachers should not consider themselves professional counselors, listening may help parents find the answer to their problem.

Reflective listening when a parent expresses concerns may allow the parent to hear the way the teacher heard and interpreted the message. Teachers can provide parents opportunities to express themselves, communicate openly and freely about their children's problems, and maintain a partnership with the teacher. Impromptu conferences need *not* be negative interactions. When teachers develop and maintain open-minded attitudes and express mutual concern for the child involved, many problems are alleviated.

Parents often meet with teachers in unscheduled conferences to feel that they can exercise some control over the educational process. At times, parents are also insecure and perceive themselves as having an advantage when meeting without prior notice. In these instances it is best to allow them to express feelings, ventilate, and ask questions. When responding to them, consider their perspective, use wait time to think and organize your answer, then respond. If you do not have an answer—say just that. Teachers do not have all the answers and should not feel obligated to create them. Sometimes when parents see that the teacher is uncertain of the answer about a concern or problem, they develop further respect for the teacher's thoughtful sincerity. When teachers express open, honest, mutual concern and make efforts to investigate the issue and respond at a later time, parents are more satisfied than they would have been with an immediate solution. Often teachers may involve parents in the search for the solution or alternative. Parents may express respect for the teacher who asks for time to consider, investigate, and meet again with them.

It may be painful for a parent to acknowledge that a child has a problem. This concern may be expressed in anger or an accusatory tone (47). In this circumstance it is important for the teacher to focus on the problem rather than responding to the parent's anger. Consider the parent's feelings, interpret the anger as concern, and respond in a relaxed manner.

At this point in the conference it is critical that the teacher be aware of his/her attitude and response. Too relaxed a response may portray an air of unconcern. Too hasty a response may cause the parent to interpret the teacher's attitude as arrogant. The timing and nature of the response are crucial. It is best to use wait time and/or ask for an additional meeting to provide valid, sincere alternatives in problem solving with parents. Appendix D contains additional information concerning conflict resolution.

When a parent appears to be asking, "Am I a good parent?" it is imperative that the teacher acknowledge this unvoiced question. Respond in a comforting, adult manner. Avoid giving the parent the impression that he/she is really off track and that you know it all. The message conveyed should indicate to the worried parent that "we are a team working together to investigate all angles of this issue" (47). Sometimes a word of praise, encouragement, or recognition may compliment the parent and provide support. Parents are often seeking the teacher's approval concerning their competencies and skills in parenting. Even if the teacher does not know the parent well, it is important to convey a supportive encouraging attitude toward him or her.

When parents and teachers possess conflicting values, acknowledgment and respect without agreement must be expressed. Viewpoints may be stated in nonjudgmental terms (47). It should be noted, however, that suggesting alternative measures may not always work. If the parents perceive that the teacher is criticizing their parenting style, they may become closed-minded and choose to end the conference. Some parents may be too strongly invested in their current parenting style to listen to alternative suggestions. If the teacher respects their choice *not* to listen, however, the parents may be more open to suggestions in future discussions.

# Chapter 10

# PROMOTING PARTNERSHIPS

Parent-teacher conferencing is only one facet of parent involvement. In most cases, the interactions that occur, formally or informally, between teachers and parents set the tone for future involvement of parents. When teachers possess effective communication skills and human relations skills in working with parents, more positive relationships are established between home and school.

According to Bauch:

> The family is a great source of knowledge about the child, and has already had a huge influence on the child's overall development. Since most parents are relatively unprepared to create optimal learning experiences for their young children, they need the support and interaction that can come from active participation in the work of the school. (2)

In addition, schools must recognize and applaud the home as the foundation of the child's learning. Teachers must make every effort to bridge the gap between home and school. Effective communication between teachers and parents can and will bridge that gap.

Because parents are the first teachers of young children, the family provides the greatest influence upon children's intellectual and social development (33). These important interactions between family members are crucial and teachers must be aware of them and their impact as the child comes to school with this unique background.

As Holland concluded:

> If teachers are to encourage successful parent participation, they should initiate active, personal, persistent, flexible, and positive communication efforts with parents. Teachers must

*believe* that parents are an integral part of the educational program and *expect* parents to participate. (33)

In 1987, the National Association for the Education of Young Children (NAEYC) published *Developmentally Appropriate Practice* for early childhood educators and advocates (7). These guidelines incorporate parent involvement as an integral part of the educational programs provided for young children that are "developmentally appropriate." In inappropriate practice, teachers communicate with parents *only* about problems and conflicts. Parents view teachers as experts and often feel isolated from their child's experiences. In developmentally appropriate practice, however, teachers work in partnership with parents, communicating regularly to build mutual understanding and greater consistency for all children (7).

For teachers in early childhood to achieve educational success (from a global perspective), effective meetings with parents are a must. These conferences are crucial to the success of the child, the teacher, and the school. Furthermore, they should foster parent education and effective communication between home and school, and encourage ongoing support (23). They should also "focus on the education of the child as a collaborative effort" (23). An ultimate goal of parent-teacher conferences is mutual trust and improved relationships. Effective conferences should be both productive and enlightening for all involved (22).

Parent involvement, as previously stated, is an integral part of early childhood education efforts, past and present. Possibly more than ever before, parents and educators must work together in partnership toward quality education for young children. Teachers must be more assertive in efforts to promote positive relations with parents so that optimal learning may occur. A strong partnership between home and school is essential if quality education is to be provided to all children (25).

# APPENDIXES

# A. CONFERENCE EVALUATION CHECKLIST*

*Yes*    *No*

Did you:

_____ _____ Prepare ahead by collecting ancedotal records, tests, papers, notebooks, workbooks, and/or art samples?

_____ _____ Send the parent a conference agenda (tentative)?

_____ _____ Ask for parent's input?

_____ _____ Provide exhibits, displays, or interesting reading materials for parents as they waited for their conferences?

_____ _____ Make arrangements for coffee, tea, or water for parents as they waited for their conferences?

_____ _____ Prepare your room with attractive displays of the children's work?

_____ _____ Welcome the parents with a friendly greeting at the door?

_____ _____ Sit beside the parent in adult-sized chairs?

_____ _____ Begin and end on a positive note?

_____ _____ Adjust your conference to the parents' needs and levels of understanding?

_____ _____ Develop clear objectives for the conference?

_____ _____ Say in descriptive terms what you meant, avoiding educational jargon and use of initials?

_____ _____ Listen reflectively?

_____ _____ Take notes to document and implement parental input?

---

*Adapted from "Effective Parent-Teacher Conferences: A Guide for Student Teachers," by S.D. Lawler. Peabody College of Vanderbilt University, 1987.

_____ _____ Use open, honest communication?

_____ _____ Allow the parent to talk more than 50 percent of the time?

_____ _____ Avoid comparisons of parents or children?

_____ _____ Work together to plan the child's educational program?

_____ _____ Mentally evaluate the conference as it proceeded?

_____ _____ Summarize your discussion?

_____ _____ Plan for followup communication?

# B. DISCIPLINE CONFERENCE VIGNETTE

## Situational Vignette: Dustin*

Teacher: Mrs. Center

Dustin is new in the neighborhood. He moved into the school district after school had been in session for two months. The secretary told you that he lives in the trailer park. Dustin is a confident student and often shows leadership in classroom situations and at play. When he is frustrated, he often uses profanity. You tried to ignore these outbursts, but now the other children have been running to you saying that Dustin is swearing. You are concerned that other parents will complain. You have called Dustin's mother to come in for a conference to see if you can eliminate Dustin's swearing.

Parent: Mrs. Adams

Dustin's teacher called and asked you to come in for a conference to discuss a problem. You know that something is "wrong" at school, but Mrs. Center did not tell you about the problem. She said that you could talk about it at the meeting. (This is a scary feeling for you.) You live in the trailer park and your husband is a construction worker. He often brings some of his crew home to play cards or watch football on TV. Mr. Adams likes to have Dustin hang around with the men. Although Mr. Adams works hard and is very busy, he tries to spend time with Dustin. They have a good relationship and you are proud of your family. Most people have commented that Dustin is a good boy.

Now read what happens in a meeting between a kindergarten teacher and a parent who is unaware of the problem. See if the conference is effective and if a partnership has been established when the meeting ends.

---

*Adapted from "Parent-Teacher Conference Role-Play Activities," by J. P. Bauch. Materials developed at Peabody College of Vanderbilt University, Nashville, Tenn., 1985.

*Discipline Conference Vignette:*
*Dustin*

MRS. CENTER: Mrs. Adams? I am very glad to meet you. I am Mrs. Laurie Center, Dustin's kindergarten teacher. Please call me Laurie.

MRS. ADAMS: I wanted to meet you, Laurie, but when we enrolled Dustin, my husband had to bring him. I was at work. You said that there was a problem.

MRS. CENTER: Well, Dustin is doing well in kindergarten. He has strong leadership abilities and the other children seem to like him. He learns quickly and seems attentive in storytime and during math lessons.

MRS. ADAMS: Well, that's good, but I am worried about what Dustin did wrong.

MRS. CENTER: Well, on several occasions, Dustin has been swearing. He gets angry or upset and uses profanity. As you know, I'm sure, Mrs. Adams, here at school, we *cannot* allow that sort of talk.

MRS. ADAMS: How many times has this happened?

MRS. CENTER: The first few times, I ignored it, but it has happened several more times. You see, Mrs. Adams, Dustin says that he heard the words from your husband and his friends. Dustin said that they say those words at your house and he can't understand why he isn't supposed to say them here. I am concerned that some of the other parents will complain. Several children have reported to me the exact words Dustin has used. I am afraid that their parents will complain to me and maybe even go to the principal. I hope you understand.

MRS. ADAMS: Oh, yes, Mrs. Center, I understand. You are saying that my husband and his friends should not say those words in front of Dustin. Well, let me tell you, my husband is a good father and he spends lots of time, when he can, with Dustin. If you think I intend to go home and tell Dustin's father to stop that, you have another think coming! (She rises to leave.)

MRS. CENTER: Oh, no, Mrs. Adams. I am sorry that I didn't explain myself well. I was not criticizing your husband or the time he spends with Dustin. I understand that your home life is your personal business. I meant to ask you if you could help me explain to Dustin why these words are not appropriate at school.

MRS. ADAMS: Well, Mrs. Center, you didn't say that. I will have a talk with Dustin. I'll tell him that it is best for him not to use those words so that his friends will still like him. I think things will be better. Is there anything else?

MRS. CENTER: No, Mrs. Adams. I wanted to talk to you about Dustin and to meet with you, but there are no other problems. I enjoy Dustin and believe that he is bright and that he is a real asset to our class. Do you have any other concerns?

MRS. ADAMS: No. I was really worried that Dustin had done something bad. Everyone tells me he is a good boy, but when you didn't say what the problem was, you know how mothers worry.

MRS. CENTER: Yes. I should have explained on the phone, but I thought it best for us to talk in person. Thank you for coming in. (Mrs. Adams leaves.)


Did communication occur? Was a partnership established? Were plans made for followup? Did Mrs. Center conduct an effective meeting? Will Mrs. Adams feel welcome and free to contact Mrs. Center in the future?

# C. CONFLICTING AGENDAS
# ROLE-PLAY ACTIVITIES

## The Agenda Issue: Kathy*

Instructions: Role play with a friend. Do not read the parent's role if you are prepared to play the teacher's role. Your lack of awareness of the parent's agenda will prepare you for this type of conference. Use the steps in the Lawler Model, but see what happens when the parent leads you astray.

Parent's Role

You and your husband have finally separated after three months of fighting and conflict at home. He moved out four days ago and you are really upset about it. You think you really love him, but his drinking and time away from the house have gotten to be too much. You are even afraid that he might hurt Kathy. This personal problem is heavy on your mind and you can think of nothing else. You trust the teacher and you are desperate to have someone to listen to your problems. Tell her all about it. Keep asking her what you should do. Explain how lonely you are and tell her that Kathy keeps asking, "Where's Daddy?"

Teacher's Role

This may be your last meeting with this mother, because Kathy will be moving to another school district next year. You are very worried about Kathy's academic performance. She has had real difficulty in classification of objects and seriation; she seems to know fewer words from the Dolch list than any other children; and she is particularly poor in sequencing and cutting skills. She was tested in March on the Peabody Picture Vocabulary Text (PPVT) and had an IQ equivalent of 88.

---

*Adapted from "Parent-Teacher Conferencing Role-Play Activities," by J. P. Bauch. Peabody College of Vanderbilt University, Nashville, Tenn., 1985.

You have decided to explain these academic and intellectual problems to Kathy's mother to help her work with Kathy at home. You are really busy today and have only 15 minutes for this conference. Remember, this will probably be your last meeting with Kathy's mother.

NOTE: Following your role play, discuss with your partner how well the conference proceeded. Discuss ways in which you may address parental agendas. Keep in mind that when parents arrive with a differing agenda, you will need to schedule an additional conference at a later date to discuss your prepared agenda.

## The Agenda Issue: Justin

### Justin's Mother

You have had concerns about Justin's work. He has been bringing home incomplete papers. You also have difficulty reading some of Justin's words.

You believe that Justin is very intelligent. Everyone says that he is bright. You know that he gets along well with others because you have watched him with his playmates at the After School Care Center.

You have taken Justin to the pediatrician who has recommended putting him on a strict diet to control his behavior (hyperactivity). He is to have no additives, preservatives, artifical flavorings, colorings, or sweeteners. You and your husband have decided to try this and you need to tell the teacher about it.

### Justin's First Grade Teacher

Justin has been having difficulties in reading. He appears to be very bright, but moves in his chair, leans back and usually falls over during reading group time, has not completed workbook assignments, and finishes reading tests long after the other children have completed their tests.

Justin's fine motor control is poor. His printing is barely

legible and he labors over writing assignments. Justin is eager to learn. He participates in class activities, he is well liked by his peers, and his verbal skills are excellent. He articulates well and has a good vocabulary. He is doing well in math except for a short attention span.

You would like to recommend to Justin's mother that he be tested for a possible learning disability. You would like to determine whether Justin needs special help.

NOTE: Role play the parts as they are written. Try to follow the Lawler Conference Model when the agendas of both parent and teacher differ from each other. Determine whether you should make the referral or possibly see what effect the diet might have on Justin's academic performance.

# D. THE DO'S AND DON'TS OF CONFLICT RESOLUTION

*Do's*

1. Do set the stage for working *with* rather than *against* the parent.

2. Do establish the level of performance (or behavior) that you expect and determine with the parent what is acceptable and unacceptable.

3. Do provide documentation of all incidents. (Generally there should be more than one incident if it is a behavior problem, and samples of work if it is an academic problem.)

4. Do take responsibility to act. Make alternative suggestions for accomplishing goals.

5. Do anticipate, and be prepared to cope with, defensiveness and possible hostility.

6. Do speak *softer* as the parent speaks louder.

7. Do exhaust the parent's list of complaints.

8. Do remain firm and direct. Gain the parent's respect as someone he or she can realistically trust. (This also means keeping information confidential *that should be confidential*.)

9. Do break the ice quickly by trying these questions:

   - What do you want *me* to do?
   - How would you like *me* to handle this?
   - What did your child say happened?
   - What can we do *together* ?

10. Do write down the parent's suggestions.

11. Do (always) plan some type of followup communication.

## Don'ts

1. Don't engage in diagnostics or reach for convenient labels.

2. Don't moralize. "You should," "You shouldn't" will only create hostility and communication barriers.

3. Don't defend or become defensive.

4. Don't make value judgments, such as "I think you're wrong," or "I think you're being foolish." These statements attack the parenting style and the decisions parents have the *right* to make.

5. Don't get boxed into a corner. If you have all the facts straight, your goal should be to help the child grow and change (usually behavior).

6. Don't raise your voice. Being professional means remaining calm, poised, and objective. Present the facts, but don't assign blame or accept verbal abuse.

7. Don't own problems that belong to others. (Remember Sujette and don't try to change parental style or values.)

8. Don't belittle or minimize the problem.

9. Don't *promise things you can't produce.* We all have the tendency to want to make things OK. When promises that cannot be kept are made, the results are usually loss of trust and confidence on the part of the parent.

# BIBLIOGRAPHY

1. Barron, B. G., and Colvin, J. M. "Teacher-Talk to Parents." *Education* 105, no. 4 (March 1985): 443–49.

2. Bauch, J. P. "Parent-Teacher Conferencing Role-Play Activities." Materials prepared at Peabody College of Vanderbilt University, Nashville, Tenn., 1985.

3. Bauch, J. P., ed. *Early Childhood Education in the Schools.* Washington, D.C.: National Education Association, 1988.

4. Beihler, R. F., and Snowman, J. *Psychology Applied to Teaching.* Boston: Houghton Mifflin, 1986.

5. Bell, G. E. "Making the Most of Parent-Teacher Conferences: Tips for Teachers." *ACEI Focus on Early Childhood* 2, no.1 (Fall 1989): 2.

6. Bjorklund, G., and Berger, C. "Making Conferences Work for Parents, Teachers, and Children." *Young Children,* 42, no. 2 (January 1987): 26–31.

7. Bredekamp, S., ed. *Developmentally Appropriate Practice.* Washington, D.C.: National Association for the Education of Young Children, 1987.

8. Burgess, K., and Johnston, L. "Parent-Teacher Conferences: Building a Team." Project Enlightenment. Wake County Public School System, Raleigh, N.C., 1987. ED 293 296.

9. Cooper, P. J. "Teachers as Speakers." Paper presented at the annual meeting of the Association for Teacher Educators, Atlanta, February 1986. ED 266 521.

10. Cooper, R. J., and others. "Simformation 6: Planning, Conducting, and Evaluating Parent-Teacher Conferences." National Institute of Education, Washington, D.C., January 1977. ED 208 466.

11. Ehly, S. W.; Conoley, J. C.; and Rosenthal, D. *Working with Parents of Exceptional Children.* St. Louis, Mo.: Times Mirror/ Mosby College Publishing, 1985.

12. Elksnin, L. K., and Elksnin, N. "Collaborative Consultation: Improving Parent-Teacher Communication." *Academic Therapy* 24, no. 3 (January 1989): 261–69.

13. Ellenburg, F. C., and Lanier, N. J. "Interacting Effectively with Parents." *Childhood Education* 24, no. 3 (May/June 1984): 261–69.

14. Epstein, J. L. "Parents' Reactions to Teacher Practices of Parent Involvement." *Elementary School Journal* 86 (1986): 277–94.

15. Faerstein, L. M. "Coping and Defense Mechanisms of Mothers of Learning Disabled Children." *Journal of Learning Disabilities* 19 (January 1986): 8–11.

16. _____. "Stress and Coping in Families of Learning Disabled Children: A Literature Review." *Journal of Learning Disabilities* 14 (August/September 1981): 420–30.

17. Fiscus, E., and Mandell, C. *Developing Individualized Educational Programs.* St. Paul, Minn: West, 1983.

18. Fuery, C. "Teacher Public Relations and Parents." *Momentum* 16, no. 1 (February 1985): 46–47.

19. Galinsky, E. "Parents and Teacher-Caregivers: Sources of Tension, Sources of Support." *Young Children* 43 (March 1988): 4–12.

20. Gargiulo, R. M. *Working with Parents of Exceptional Children.* Boston: Houghton Mifflin, 1985.

21. Gartner, A. "Parents, No Longer Excluded, Just Ignored: Some Ways to Do It Nicely." *Exceptional Parent* 18, no. 1 (January/February 1988): 40–41.

22. Gelfer, J. I., and Perkins, P. G. "Effective Communication with Parents." *Childhood Education* 64, no. 1 (October 1987): 19–22.

23. Gonsalves, B. B. "Call a Meeting?" *Momentum* 19, no. 4 (November 1988): 21–22.

24. Greenberg, D., and Wolf, D. "The Economic Consequences of Experiencing Parental Marital Disruptions." *Children and Youth Services Review* 4 (1982): 141–62.

25. Haley, P., and Berry, K. "Home and School as Partners: Helping Parents Help Their Children." Regional Laboratory for Educational Improvement of the Northeast and Islands, Andover, Mass., 1988. ED 293 622.

26. Hamachek, A. L., and Romano, L. G. "Focus on Parent-Teacher Conferences." Paper presented at the annual meeting of the Michigan Association of Middle School Educators, East Lansing, 1984. ED 265 131.

27. Harris and Associates. "The American Teacher 1987. Strengthening Links Between Home and School." Metropolitan Life Survey, New York, 1987. ED 289 841.

28. Hayes, C. D., and Kamerman, S. B., eds. *Children of Working Parents: Experiences and Outcomes.* Washington, D.C.: National Academy Press, 1983.

29. Hayes, R. L. "The Reconstruction of Educational Experience: The Parent Conference." *Education* 107, no. 3 (1987): 305–9.

30. Herman, J. L., and Yeh, J. P. "Some Effects of Parent Involvement in Schools." *Urban Review* 15, no. 1 (1983): 11–17.

31. Hill, M. S.; Augustiniak, S.; and Ponza, M. "The Impact of Parental Marital Disruption on the Socio-Economic Attainments of Children as Adults." Unpublished manuscript. University of Michigan, Ann Arbor, Research Center, 1985.

32. Hofferth, S. L. "Implications of Family Trends for Children: A Research Perspective." *Educational Leadership* (February 1987): 78–84.

33. Holland, K. E. "Parents and Teachers: Can Home and School Literacy Boundaries Be Broken?' Unpublished manuscript. Education in Appalachia, 1987. ED 300 182.

34. Hunter, M., and Lawrence, G. "Staff Meeting: Madeline Hunter Discusses Parent Conferences." *Instructor* 83 (February 1974): 18.

35. Idol, L.; Paolucci-Whitcomb, P.; and Nevin, A. *Collaborative Consultation.* Austin, Texas: PRO-ED, 1986.

36. *Instructor.* "How to Talk to Parents and Get the Message Across." 93, no. 4 (November/December 1983): 64–66.

37. Johns Hopkins University. "A Study of Teacher Practices of Parent Involvement: Results from Surveys of Teachers and Parents." Baltimore: Center for Social Organization of Schools, 1983. ED 238 558.

38. Ladner, J. "Providing a Healthy Environment for Interracial Children." *Interracial Books for Children Bulletin* 15, no. 6 (1984): 13–15.

39. Lawler, S. D. "The Lawler Model for Effective Parent-Teacher Conferences." Arkansas State University, Jonesbaro, 1990.

40. ____. "Effective Parent-Teacher Conferences: A Guide for Student Teachers." Peabody College of Vanderbilt University, 1987. ED 313 125.

41. Leeper, S. H.; Witherspoon, R. L.; and Day, B. "Involving Parents as Partners." *Good Schools for Young Children.* 5th ed. New York: Macmillan, 1984.

42. Littleton, M. "Effective Parent-Teacher Conferences." *Catalyst for Change* 15, no. 1 (Fall 1985): 12–14.

43. Manning, M. L. "The Involved Father: A New Challenge in Parent Conferences." *Clearing House* 57, no. 1 (September 1983): 17–19.

44. McLanahan, S. "Family Structure and the Reproduction of Poverty." *American Journal of Sociology* 90 (1986): 873–901.

45. McSweeney, J. P. "Five Guidelines for Parent-Teacher Conferences." *Clearing House* 56, no. 7 (March 1983): 319–20.

46. Miller, B. I. "Parental Involvement Affects Reading Achievement of First, Second, and Third Graders." Exit Project, Indiana University at South Bend, 1986. ED 279 997.

47. Morgan, E. L. "Talking with Parents When Concerns Come Up." *Young Children* 44, no. 2 (January 1989): 52–56.

48. Morrison, G. S. *Early Childhood Education Today.* 4th ed. Columbus: Merrill Publishing Co., 1988.

49. Norton, R. *Communicator Style Theory, Applications, and Measures.* Beverly Hills: Sage, 1983.

50. Perkins, J., and Buchanan, A. "How Parents Find Out About Student Progress." Southwest Regional Laboratory for Educational Research and Development, Los Alamitos, Calif., 1983. ED 250 787.

51. Peters, D. L.; Neisworth, J. T.; and Yawkey, T. D. *Early Childhood Education: From Theory to Practice.* Monterey, Calif.: Brooks/Cole, 1985.

52. Price, B. J., and Marsh, G. E. "Practical Suggestions for Planning and Conducting Parent Conferences." *Teaching Exceptional Children* 17, no. 4 (Summer 1985): 274–78.

53. Readdick, C. A.; Golbeck, S. L.; Klein, E. L.; and Cartwright, C. A. "The Child-Parent-Teacher Conference." *Young Children* 39, no. 5 (July 1984): 67–73.

54. Reddick, T. L., and Peach, L. E. "A Study of Methods of School-Community Communications Based on Responses of Parents of School Children in Middle Tennessee." Paper presented at the annual meeting of the Mid-South Educational Research Association, Mobile, Ala., November 1987. ED 294 321.

55. Reiss, E. M. "Conferencing Skills: Working with Parents." *Clearing House* 62, no. 2 (October 1988): 81–83.

56. Roberds-Baxter, S. "The Parent Connection: Enhancing the Affective Component of Parent Conferences." *Teaching Exceptional Children* 17, no. 1 (Fall 1984): 55–58.

57. Scheerschmidt, A. E. "The Suspicion of a Learning Disability: A Guide for the Parent-Teacher Conference." Unpublished manuscript, 1986. ED 295 374.

58. Seefeldt, C. *Teaching Young Children.* New York: Prentice Hall, 1984.

59. Shapiro, J., and Doiron, R. "Literacy Environments: Bridging the Gap Between Home and School." *Childhood Education* 63 no.4 (April 1987): 263–69.

60. Shea, T. M., and Bauer, A. M. *Parents and Teachers of Exceptional Students.* Boston: Allyn and Bacon, 1985.

61. Swap, S. M. *Enhancing Parent Involvement in Schools*. New York: Teachers College Press, 1987.

62. Swick, K. J., and Duff, R. E. *The Parent-Teacher Bond: Relating, Responding, Rewarding*. Dubuque, Iowa: Kendall/Hunt, 1978.

63. Vaughn, S.; Bos, C. S.; Harrell, J. E.; and Lasky, B. A. "Parent Participation in the Initial Placement/IEP Conference Ten Years After Mandated Involvement." *Journal of Learning Disabilities* 21, no. 2 (February 1988): 82–89.

64. Wardle, F. "Are You Sensitive to Interracial Children's Special Identity Needs?" *Young Children* 42 (January 1987): 53–59.

65. Washington, V. "Trends in Early Childhood Education—Part I: Demographics." *Dimensions* 16, no. 2 (1988): 4–8.

66. Williams, D. L.; Chavkin, N. F.; and Stallworth, J. T. "Parent Involvement in Education: What a Survey Reveals." Paper presented for the National Coalition for Title I, Chapter I Parents' Eleventh Annual In-Service Training Conference, Crystal City, Va., October 1984.

67. Wimpelberg, R. K. "Parental Control in Public Education: The Preferences and Behaviors of Parents Related to Their Children's Schooling." Paper presented at the annual meeting of the American Educational Research Association, Los Angeles, 1981. ED 208 514.

68. Zuga, K. F. "How Do Parent-Teacher Conferences Influence the Curriculum?" Paper presented at the annual meeting of the American Educational Research Association, Montreal, Canada, April 1983. ED 233 435.

# ADDITIONAL RESOURCES

Barron, B. "Invite Adults to School for a Parent-Teacher Conference." *Executive Educator* 5, no. 12 (1983): 24–25.

Becker, H. J., and Epstein, J. L. "Parent Involvement: A Survey of Teacher Practices." *Elementary School Journal* 83, no. 2 (1982): 85–102.

Berger, E. H. *Parents as Partners in Education.* 2d ed. St. Louis, Mo.: Mosby, 1987.

Brown, L., and Jalongo, M. R. "Make Parent-Teacher Conferences Better." Professional Report No. 241. Largo, Fla.: Careers, 1986.

Cattermole, J., and Robinson, N. "Effective Home-School Communication from the Parents' Perspective." *Phi Delta Kappa* 64 (1985): 49–50.

Davis, D. H., and David, D. M. "Managing Parent-Teacher Conferences." *Today's Education* (Gen. ed.) 70 (April/May 1981): 46–50.

Elkind, D. *Miseducation.* New York: Knopf, 1989.

Epstein, J. L. "What Principals Should Know About Parent Involvement." *Principal* (January 1987): 6–9.

Fischer, K. W., and Lazerson, A. *Human Development.* New York: W. H. Freeman, 1984.

Frost, J. L. "Children in a Changing Society." *Childhood Education* (March/April 1986): 242–49.

Gotts, E. E., and Purnell, R. F. *Improving Home-School Communication.* Bloomington, Ind.: Phi Delta Kappa Educational Foundation, 1985.

Henderson, A. T.; Marburger, C. L.; and Ooms, T. "Building a Family-School Relationship." *Principal* (January 1987): 12–15.

Isenberg, J. "Societal Influences on Children." *Childhood Education* 63, no. 5 (June 1987): 341–48.

Kahn, A. P. "Our School or Yours?" *Principal* (January 1987): 10–11.

Ladner, J. "Providing a Healthy Environment for Interracial Children." *Interracial Books for Children Bulletin* 15, no. 6 (1984): 13–15.

Lightfoot, S. L. "Toward Conflict Resolution: Relationships Between Families and Schools." *Theory into Practice* 20, no. 2 (1981): 97–104.

Long, L. "Parents: The Untapped Resource." *Momentum* 13, no. 3 (1982): 21–22.

Manning, M. L. "The Involved Father: A New Challenge in Parent Conferences." *Clearing House* 57, no. 7 (1983): 319–20.

Mcloughlin, C. S. *Parent-Teacher Conferencing.* Springfield, Ill.: Charles C. Thomas, 1987.

Meddin, B. J., and Rosen, A. L. "Child Abuse and Neglect: Prevention and Reporting." *Young Children* 41, no. 4 (May 1986): 26–30.

Meier, J. H. "Corporal Punishment in the Schools." *Childhood Education* 58, no. 4 (May 1986): 26–30.

Pennsylvania Department of Education. "Teacher's Guide to Parent Involvement." *Pennsylvania Education* 17, no. 6 (April 1986): 1–12.

Ross, D. D., and Bondy, E. "Communicating with Parents About Beginning Reading Instruction." *Childhood Education* 63, no. 4 (April 1987): 270–74.

Rotter, J. C., and Robinson, E. H. *Parent-Teacher Conferencing.* Washington, D.C.: National Education Association, 1986.

Simmons, B., and Brewer, J. "When Parents of Kindergartners Ask 'Why?'" *Childhood Education* 61 (1985): 177–84.

Skeen, P., and McKenry, P. C. "The Teacher's Role in Facilitating a Child's Adjustment to Divorce." *Young Children* 35, no. 5 (July 1980): 3–12.

Swick, K. J. *Inviting Parents into the Young Child's World.* Champaign, Ill.: Stipes Publishing Co., 1984.

Tizard, J. "Collaborating Between Teachers and Parents in Assisting Children's Reading." *British Journal of Educational Psychology* 52 (February 1982): 1–15.

Wayson, W.; DeVoss, G.; Kaeser, S.; Lasley, T.; and Pinnell, G. *Handbook for Developing Schools with Good Discipline.* Bloomington, Ind.: Phi Delta Kappa, 1982.

Williams, D. K. *Handbook for Involving Parents in Education.* Atlanta: Humanics Ltd., 1985.

Wilson, J.; Pentecoste, J.; and Nelms, C. "The Effects of Age, Occupation, Race and Education on Parent Communication." *Education* 103, no. 4 (1983): 402–4.